TOY FARMER

March 1997
$3.50

ERTL'S PRECISION SERIES
OLIVER 77 ROW CROP

ARCADE

Ford Sedans, Ford Tourings,
Ford Coupes, Fordson Tractors, Oliver Plows, W. & K.
Truck Trailers, Yellow Cabs,
Andy Gump 348 and Chester
in Pony Cart. Only a few of
the famous Arcade cast iron
toys—by far the favorites of
children everywhere.

Dealers: These toys are perfect miniature reproductions of
the "real ones". *Wonderful advertising novelties for you.*
Write for catalog. Your jobber can supply you.

ARCADE MANUFACTURING CO.
FREEPORT ` ` ` ILLINOIS

TOYS

Toy Farm Tractors

Text by Bill Vossler
Photographs by Andy Kraushaar
Foreword by Claire D. Scheibe, *Toy Farmer* Magazine

Voyageur Press
A TOWN SQUARE BOOK

Edited by Michael Dregni
Designed by Andrea Rud
Printed in Hong Kong

First Hardcover Edition
98   99   00   01   02   5   4   3   2   1
First Paperback Edition
00   01   02   03   04   5   4   3   2   1

Library of Congress Cataloging-in-Publication Data
Vossler, Bill, 1946–
      Toy farm tractors : an entertaining history of toy tractors and toy farm collectibles / text by Bill Vossler; foreword by Claire Scheibe ; photographs by Andy Kraushaar.
        p.   cm.
      "A Town Square book."
      Includes bibliographical references and index.
      ISBN 0-89658-380-5
      ISBN 0-89658-511-5 (alk. paper)
        1. Farm tractors—Models—Collectors and collecting—History. 2. Toys—Collectors and collecting—
History. I. Title.

TL233.8.V6723 2000
629.22'152'075—dc21   00-031987
                                                    CIP

Published by Voyageur Press, Inc.
123 North Second Street, P.O. Box 338
Stillwater, MN 55082 U.S.A.
651-430-2210, fax 651-430-2211
books@voyageurpress.com
www.voyageurpress.com

Distributed in Europe by Midland Publishing Ltd.
Unit 3, Maizefield, Hinckley Fields
Leicester LE10 1YF, England
01455 233 747, fax 01455 233 737, E-mail:
midlandbooks@compuserve.com

Page 1: Top, *This pair of 1/16 Massey Harris 44 tractors was manufactured by the Slik-Toy Company of Lansing, Iowa. Collection: State Historical Society of Wisconsin.* Bottom left, Toy Farmer *magazine from March 1997 featuring Ertl's Precision Series Oliver 77 Row Crop.* Bottom right, *Arcade toy farm tractor advertisement from 1924.*

On the title pages: *Ertl built this 1/16 John Deere Model A tractor in 1947. The Ertl tractor used Arcade front wheels purchased from Arcade after the firm went bankrupt. The tractor was made of sand-cast aluminum and is pulling a 1/16 John Deere spreader made from pressed steel by Carter for Eska in 1950. This spreader has rubber wheels and short levers. Collection: State Historical Society of Wisconsin.*

Acknowledgments

This book may attempt to do the impossible. In it, I have tried to cover every aspect of the farm toy world. It certainly discusses subjects that most farm toy books and publications generally gloss over, like fraud, or the materials from which farm toys are made.

On the other hand, this book also discusses, through the words of collectors and people who know farm toys, all the well-loved aspects of the farm toy world, from farm toy shows to farm toy museums.

Where this book has failed, I must take blame. Where it has succeeded, credit must go to other people.

No book writes itself, and this book is no different. It is the result of many hours of work and a great deal of unselfish giving, most notably by Rick Campbell of Apple River, Illinois; Dick Sonnek of Mapleton, Minnesota; Eldon Trumm of Worthington, Iowa; and Ken Updike of Evansville, Wisconsin.

Many thanks to all the people who "wanted to help a little"—a euphemism for doing a lot of hard work to make sure this book is accurate. On this score, I owe thanks to the people mentioned above, as well as to Al of Al's Farm Toys of Bloomington, Minnesota.

I also want to thank Claire D. Scheibe of *Toy Farmer* magazine in LaMoure, North Dakota.

Unless otherwise noted, the farm toys pictured are from the collection of the National Farm Toy Museum in Dyersville, Iowa. I want to thank the other collectors and institutions who allowed their farm toys to be photographed: Sigrid Arnott of Minneapolis, Minnesota; Lewis P. Checchia of The Franklin Mint; Jim Goke of St. Cloud, Minnesota; Brad Johnson of Red Wing, Minnesota; Ray Lacktorin of White Bear Lake, Minnesota; Brent Peterson of the Washington County Historical Society, Stillwater, Minnesota; and the State Historical Society of Wisconsin, Madison.

And most of all, thanks to my superb editor, Michael Dregni.

Bill Vossler

Scale Models White Field Boss 185
Scale Models of Dyersville, Iowa, manufactured this 1/16 White Field Boss 185 from die-cast steel in 1988. This steerable model is a "First Edition"; often only one is given to each dealer, and thus the number made is small, and the tractors are often rare.

Contents

1929 Marx tin-toy crawler

Toy Farmer magazine

Ertl Antique Series John Deere G

Mickey Mouse tractors

Classic 1965 Ertl catalog

1921 Sears Roebuck toy tractor and implements

Foreword

By Claire D. Scheibe, *Toy Farmer* Magazine

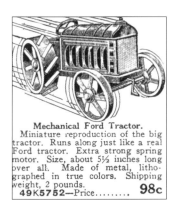

Mechanical Ford Tractor.
Miniature reproduction of the big tractor. Runs along just like a real Ford tractor. Extra strong spring motor. Size, about 5½ inches long over all. Made of metal, lithographed in true colors. Shipping weight, 2 pounds.
49K5752—Price......... **98c**

Golden fields of grain under a scorching sun and days of feeding and nursing livestock through the long days of winter seem far away, yet they make up part of the background of the average farm toy collector.

In our childhood, many of us had varied interests nurtured by visits to the neighborhood farm equipment dealer or to a relative's farm. As we grew in age, so did our interest in farm models.

As more and more people became interested in farm toys, the closet collector knew he or she could step forth. Farm toy collections began to show up in living rooms around the nation, and the collecting of those farm models that held fond memories of times past became accepted, and transformed bygone days into living memories.

At home and around the world, farm toy collecting has established itself into a well-respected and well-known hobby. It is my hope that Bill Vossler will guide you through the history of farm toy collecting and give you an understanding of the pleasures enjoyed by the farm model hobbyist.

The pages of this book share the story of different farm toy collectors and the history of the farm toy hobby. Our hope is that through this book you will share the enjoyment to a point of going forth and finding some examples of times gone by.

"Mechanical Ford Tractor" advertisement
Above: *The 1922 Sears, Roebuck and Company catalog contained this "Mechanical Ford Tractor," which was billed as a "miniature reproduction of the big tractor." This toy measured about 5½ inches long (138 mm) and sold for ninety-eight cents.*

Product Miniature Ford 8N
Facing page: *Product Miniature (PM) of Milwaukee, Wisconsin, made this 1/12 Ford Ferguson N Series tractor from plastic in the early 1950s. Collection: State Historical Society of Wisconsin.*

Chapter 1

Farm Toys: As Old As Farming

Farm toys have probably existed since the planting of the first crops. The earliest farm toys were not made by large companies as they are today; they were not produced by companies at all, but by young farm boys and girls who watched their fathers and mothers rake hay or thresh wheat and wanted a rig just like their parents' to emulate their work. The first farm toys may also have been lovingly made as gifts from a father or mother to a child. Until the nineteenth century, all toys were handmade.

The earliest known farm toy was a small cart and plow created for the children of Edward I, King of England in the late thirteenth century. It is likely that other farm toys were made earlier, yet were not recorded or did not survive.

The first known commercial farm toys were not manufactured in North America until the late 1800s. This was due as much to the infancy of the toy-making industry as to the ingrained Puritan ethic. Joseph Doucette and C. L. Collins wrote in *Collecting Antique Toys* that before 1860, the United States "was still fairly well caught up in the Puritan work ethic, and play was thought to be non-productive. To be successful, one had to work every day and save one's hard-earned money. Since no laws were in effect to protect children, they were forced to work alongside adults. Children were considered to be miniature adults and were treated as such. In fact, until the late 1860s, toys were usually used to teach moral lessons rather than to divert children." The workload for children as well as adults on American and Canadian farms kept their hands busy with real farm equipment and left little time to play with toy versions.

Even if farm toys had been commercially available in the early to mid-1800s, parents and kids probably would not have thought of buying the miniature machinery—or been able to afford it. They grew up at a time when you made what you needed, or made do with what you had. So, these hard-working adults and kids carved toys from wood with a jackknife, fashioned them from corn husks, or crafted them from spare metal or other items. They found old thread for horse reins, wood knots for wheels, and made use of whatever else was handy to create the parts they needed. The identical process was repeated decades later during the Great Depression of the 1930s, a time when many wonderful farm toys were being commercially manufactured. Most farm kids, however, could not afford these company-made toys; instead, these resourceful boys and girls used bottle caps for wheels, cardboard for tractor bodies, discarded nails for axles—whatever worked. Carlyle Greibrok is a farm toy collector and owner of the Mini-History Farm and County Fair Museum of rural Austin, Minnesota. He remembers building farm tractors and machinery out of cardboard: "We took the cardboard off the back of a paper writing tablet and used a piece of wire, part of a pencil, or a Tinkertoy to make the axles. It wasn't great, but it killed time during the long winter evenings." Greibrok made his own miniature Fordsons and International 10/20s, the tractors that were popular at the time.

Homemade toys rarely lasted long, of course, because these children of the 1800s, and their Great Depression–era successors, played hard with the toys in their miniature fields in the shade of elm trees during their rare free moments. Youngsters often broke their toys, or crippled them badly, so that few, if any, of the homemade toys survive today.

To weather decades of use was not the most important criteria for building these toys—nor was the thought of collecting them. Children did not craft the toys to be set on shelves to preserve them. Rather, they were built for present fun, for the joy of practicing how to farm. In a sense, children playing with homemade farm toys was similar to kittens attacking a ball of yarn: Both were preparing for their adult future.

The Rise of Commercial Farm Toys

The names of the little boys and girls who created the first farm toys in North America have been lost forever. But the children's legacy has not. Today, thou-

Slik Massey-Harris 44
Previous page: *This pair of 1/16 Massey Harris 44 tractors was manufactured by the Slik-Toy Company of Lansing, Iowa, with narrow front wheels in 1950. A companion tractor to these featured the silver driver wearing merely a cap, while the drivers on these tractors were wearing pith helmets. The wheel rims were made of tin. Collection: State Historical Society of Wisconsin.*

Homemade wooden thresher

This wooden model of a Minnesota Chief thresher was crafted by hand as a toy in 1877. The original thresher was made by the Northwest Thresher Company of Stillwater, Minnesota. This toy was believed to have been made in Stillwater and is photographed on the site of the factory. Collection: Washington County Historical Society. (Photograph by Michael Dregni)

Sears steam tractors advertisement

These steam tractor farm toys from the 1922 Sears, Roebuck and Company catalog were "accurate in detail and proportion. Brass boiler, handsome gunmetal finish. Flywheel has nickeled face." The chain drive actually worked. They weighed 3–4½ pounds (1.35–2 kg) and sold for $3.98 to $6.98.

Horsedrawn farm wagon advertisements

Right, top: *In 1921 Sears, Roebuck and Company offered these horse-drawn farm wagons. The Butler Brothers mail-order catalog (later known as City Products Corporation) sold papier-mâché horses pulling hay carts in 1914, which were early forerunners of farm toys. Butler sold a variety of imported papier-mâché animals that were billed as being "practically indestructible." These toys included horses, donkeys, cows, and sheep. Butler also sold cast-iron horse-and-hay wagon combinations.*

Wilkins hay tedder advertisement

Right, bottom: *The Wilkins Toy Company of Keene, New Hampshire, offered this cast-iron No. 405 horse-drawn hay tedder in the 1880s and 1890s. It measured 9½ inches (238 mm) long.*

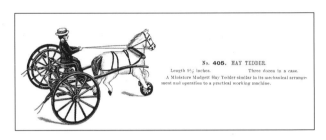

sands of youngsters—and many grownups—play with commercially manufactured farm toys with features that replicate their parents' real farm machinery. The early homemade toys inspired commercial manufacture of farm toys by a few farsighted firms beginning in the late 1800s and blossoming in the 1900s. Today, mass-produced miniature tractors and other agricultural implements are crafted by a variety of companies around the world and are available to fans everywhere.

Like the history of the creators of the first homemade toys, the history of the pioneering toy manufacturers is also largely lost. As Doucette and Collins wrote, "Tracing the birth of the toy industry is somewhat impossible, since many, if not most, old records have been lost through indifference or natural calamities, such as fire. Unfortunately, the complete and true story of where the first toys were manufactured and mass-produced in this country will probably never be known." However, much can be deduced by studying old catalogs, magazine advertisements, rare brochures, and the toys themselves.

The earliest known commercially manufactured North American toy is believed by toy historians to be a horse-drawn fire pumper wagon with a tin boiler and pump apparatus made in 1840 by the firm Francis, Field & Francis of Philadelphia. The toy was fashioned from a variety of materials: The horses were made of formed tin, the wheels cast in iron, and the first

Vindex Deere tractor and plow advertisement

Vindex offered this No. 81 Deere tractor in green or yellow with removable nickel-plated driver as well as a Deere three-bottom plow in the 1920s.

Gibbs horse-drawn farm wagon

This pair of Gibbs horses pulls a wagonload of farm produce, which includes milk, apples, and other products. The faded writing on the side of the wagon reads "Black Beauty Pacers," which refers to the horses, one of Gibbs's well-known toys. (Photograph by Bill Vossler)

Vindex horse-drawn hay rack

Vindex toys were made by the National Sewing Machine Company of Belvidere, Illinois. This 1/16 cast-iron Vindex farm toy consists of three parts: the pair of black horses; the bottom red gear, which was made for a John Deere hay rack (as in this picture) or grain box; and the hay rack itself. The driver did not originally accompany this toy. (Photograph by Bill Vossler)

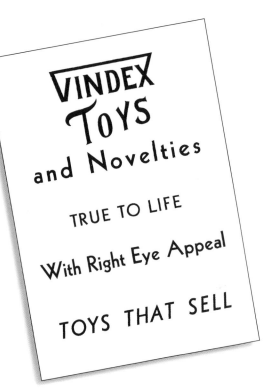

Above: **1920s Vindex advertisement**

Vindex Case L
Below: *This 1/16 cast-iron Vindex Case L tractor was one of many toys produced by the National Sewing Machine Company in 1930. It was originally gray with its obvious red wheels and in excellent condition sells in the 1990s for more than $900. (Photograph by Bill Vossler)*

Arcade Farmall M
The Arcade Manufacturing Company of Freeport, Illinois, made this 1/16 Farmall M cast-iron tractor in 1940. This tractor had a separate, plated driver; a sister tractor made a year later included a driver cast into the tractor.

engine was a combination of wood and tin.

The first commercially produced farm toys are believed to be those manufactured by the Wilkins Toy Company of Keene, New Hampshire, beginning in about 1886. Wilkins designed and cast from iron a horse-drawn mower, sulky plow, hay rake, and tedder, which spreads out new-mown hay.

The Wilkins horse-drawn farm implements were exacting replicas of the real equipment. Unfortunately, many early toy-makers did not worry about crafting faithful miniatures: Many other early cast-iron farm toys were crudely made. Even some of the toys in greatest demand—such as some of the famous 1930s Vindex toys made by the National Sewing Machine Company of Belvidere, Illinois—do not have much detail, which, along with their high prices, deters some present-day collectors from buying them.

Peculiarly, after Wilkins's began manufacturing farm toys in 1886, few farm toys showed up in the annals during the next thirty-five years. Some were found in catalogs: For example, in 1894, the famous mail-order catalog from Montgomery Ward & Company of Chicago offered a variety of toy horse-drawn wagons pulled by "natural skin" animals like those used on the farm. Montgomery Ward, as well as Sears, Roebuck and Company of Chicago and other mail-order catalogs, offered the occasional farm toy between 1886 and 1905, whether it was a farm set, farm animals, wagons, or eventually, steam traction engines and tractors. In 1914, Sears offered a steam traction engine for $4.25, and the Butler Brothers of New York City offered a variety of horses and wagons.

The Golden Age of Farm Toys

It was not until the 1920s that farm toys were made in large numbers. In 1920, the Hubley Manufacturing Com-

pany of Lancaster, Pennsylvania, cast a 4½-inch-long (112-mm) Avery 18/36 tractor, and the Arcade Manufacturing Company of Freeport, Illinois, created a two-bottom pull-type cast-iron plow (another reference states that the Arcade plow was not manufactured until 1926). These classic farm toys are highly sought after today.

These pioneering farm toys found markets, and Arcade and Hubley soon expanded their lines to become the major farm toy manufacturers during the 1920s. The Kenton Hardware Company of Kenton, Ohio, made a few farm wagons during the 1920s. The Vindex toys produced by the National Sewing Machine Company of Belvidere, Illinois, entered the market in the 1930s. Also in the 1930s, the successor to the Wilkins firm, the Kingsbury Manufacturing Company of Keene, New Hampshire, manufactured farm toys, including a 19-inch-long (475-mm) cattle truck as well as a tractor and cart made of tin, with an iron driver and white rubber wheels. Kingsbury also made a red-and-yellow two-seat cart pulled by a white goat.

Few new companies entered the toy marketplace during the Great Depression of the 1930s and during World War II, but in 1945, Fred Ertl Sr. started making farm toys in his home furnace in Dubuque, Iowa. Ertl was at the forefront of a golden age for the manufacture of farm toys that blossomed in the 1950s. This was a true golden age not only because many companies took up the re-frain, but also because some of these companies were unique and creative. Among these were Reuhl Products of Madison, Wisconsin, which created educational, well-made, take-apart farm toys; the Auburn Rubber Company of Auburn, Indiana, which mass produced rubber farm toys, especially tractors; and Carter Tru-Scale Products of Rockford, Illinois. All of these companies—and especially Reuhl and Tru-Scale—differed from their competitors in that they crafted farm toys primarily for the love and joy of making the toys.

Since the 1950s, many companies have joined the ranks of farm toy makers. In addition, farm toys are now customized and scratchbuilt in great detail and quality by many enthusiasts. The farm toy has come a long way since the plain, homemade toys of the 1800s.

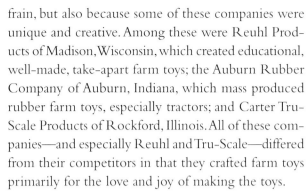

Ertl Allis-Chalmers WC
Left: *This is the toy that sparked the farm toy revolution. This was the first farm toy produced by Fred Ertl Sr. in 1945. This 1/16 Allis-Chalmers WC was made of sand-cast aluminum in the household furnace of Ertl's Dubuque, Iowa, home. In the 1990s, the tractor is worth $750. Collection: Rick Campbell. (Photograph by Bill Vossler)*

Marx Fordson advertisement

Right: *"Own a tractor of your own. Just like your Daddy's."* The 1924 Sears Roebuck catalog offered this tin wind-up Fordson made by Louis Marx & Company of New York, New York. The catalog text described the tractor as *"a regular little beauty with its bright colored wheels and reproduction of the engine on both sides of the hood."* Montgomery Ward & Company sold a similar *"Marx Guaranteed Toy"* Fordson in 1930 with a wagon, disc harrow, and rake. The tractor contained the *"Marx unbreakable spring"* clockwork wind-up motor.

100,000 Kiddies Bought This Beautiful Mechanical Tractor Last Year.

A Real Fordson in Miniature.

The New Improved Bing Tractor.

89c

Own a tractor of your own. Just like your Daddy's. A regular little beauty with its bright colored wheels and reproduction of the engine on both sides of its hood. A real miniature of a big tractor. Has a driver and runs along like a real Fordson Tractor. Notches in front axle so that you can regulate size of circle tractor runs in. Size, about 8½ inches long over all. Made of metal, lithographed in true colors. Hook at back for pulling little wagons, etc. Shipping weight, 2 pounds.

49T5752 . . . . **89c**

Ertl *Green Acres* Fordson

Left: *TV's* Green Acres *was certainly the place to be, and in 1969, the Ertl Company of Dyersville, Iowa, began making this 1/16 Fordson F die-cast tractor to commemorate the use of the same tractor in the television show. "This is an actual scale model,"* the literature read, *"of the one driven by Eddie Albert and Eva Gabor on the television show." Unfortunately, Ertl did not offer an Arnold replica.*

WE — and all the folks in Hooterville — are welcomed into millions of homes each week on CBS - TV . . . Making more and more friends for . . .

OLIVER WENDELL DOUGLAS (Eddie Albert)

ARNOLD (Himself)

LISA (Eva Gabor)

"GREEN ACRES"

NO. 850

NO. 850 FORDSON TRACTOR
. . . as seen on "Green Acres" . . . this die cast metal beauty is a blueprint replica of an antique Fordson tractor. This is an actual scale model of the one driven by Eddie Albert and Eva Gabor on the television show "Green Acres." Tractor is steerable with knee action front wheels. Die cast wheels. Painted red with gray body.
L. 6⅝", W. 3¾", H. 3¾".
Display packed — 6 per 11 lb. ctn.

NO. 5008

NO. 5008 DELUXE GREEN ACRES SET
This all metal deluxe Green Acres Set includes Oliver 1850 tractor, a flare box wagon, spreader, plow and disc. Packed in a display carton telling the Green Acres story.
L. 18½", W. 13¾", H. 5⅞".
Display packed — 3 per 14.75 lb. ctn.

NO. 5004

NO. 5004 MINI GREEN ACRES SET
This all metal Green Acres mini set is loaded with "REAL FUN." This set includes tractor, wagon, spreader, plow, disc. This one is sure to be a winner. Painted green.
L. 18½", W. 12¼", H. 4⅛".

20

Matchbox Claas combine

Above: *Lesney of England made this Matchbox Claas combine in 1967. The yellow plastic blades and front wheels rotated. The combine measured 3 inches (75 mm) long. Collection: State Historical Society of Wisconsin.*

Right: **1920s Kingsbury catalog**

Kingsbury Joys

SPEED
POWER
ENDURANCE
BEAUTY

200 FIFTH AVE · NEW YORK CITY

Ertl catalog
By 1968, Ertl offered a full range of tractors, implements, accessories, farm trucks, and pedal tractors.

Ertl Co-op E2
Ertl manufactured this die-cast 1/16 Co-op E2 tractor in 1989 as part of the 4th Dyersville Museum set. Collection: National Farm Toy Museum.

Ertl Ford 901

Above: *Ertl made this 1/16 die-cast Ford 901 Select-O-Speed tractor in 1996. The separate farmer sitting at the controls is called a "Jim Babcock" figure.*

Scale Models White 2-155

Right: *Scale Models of Dyersville, Iowa, made this 1/16 die-cast White 2-155 tractor in 1981. Note the red identification decal: Scale Models made an earlier identical White 2-155 in 1980, but it featured a silver identification decal.*

Sales sample Fergusons
These 1940s 1/16 Ferguson replicas were sales samples for Harry Ferguson's real, full-size tractors. Ferguson salespeople would show these models to potential buyers in lieu of the actual tractors during their travels around the United States and Canada. They were donated to the State Historical Society of Wisconsin in 1948 by the Ford Motor Company and the Nagel-Hart Tractor Company. Collection: State Historical Society of Wisconsin.

John Deere collector

Right: *Collector Richard Neuzil of Dyersville, Iowa, enjoys a few moments of solitude while holding an Ertl-made 1/16 die-cast John Deere 4450 tractor with a strobe decal that was offered in 1979.*

Pullmaster John Deere A

Below: *Pullmaster of Denmark made this plastic 1/16 John Deere A . Many foreign companies make John Deere toys, some licensed by Deere & Company like this one, and some not. Collection: Eldon Trumm.*

Carter Tru-Scale Farmall M
Above: *Carter Tru-Scale Products of Rockford, Illinois, manufactured this 1/16 Farmall M with yellow rims from sand-cast aluminum in 1950. This self-steering tractor is worth about $200 in excellent condition; the original product box more than doubles the value, however, to about $440.*

Gilson Riecke John Deere A
Overleaf: *This 1/16 John Deere Model A with narrow front was custom-built by Gilson Riecke of Ruthven, Iowa, in 1991. Riecke's highly detailed farm toys are in great demand. Riecke also made the attached three-bottom pull-type plow. Collection: Eldon Trumm.*

Cathy and Claire Scheibe

If it was not for Claire Scheibe, farm toys might still be traded among a few hardcore collectors and would never have become as popular as they are. One newspaper reporter even wrote recently that farm toys are "hip."

Claire and Cathy Scheibe owned and operated a small grain and cow-calf operation near LaMoure, North Dakota. The farm had been in the Scheibe family for forty years and had been started by Claire's father, Ernest. Although the farm work kept the Scheibe family busy, they established S&S Antiques as a way to supplement their income. While attending antique shows in the 1970s, Claire always kept an eye out for farm toys, particularly the ones that he had had as a child. "At that time, you weren't offered one item," Claire remembers. "It was by the boxful."

He sorted through the boxes of old Arcade, Hubley, and Vindex toys to find the ones he wanted and put the rest up for sale. Along the way, he met other collectors who shared an interest in old farm toys. "Pretty soon I was known as the toy tractor guy in North Dakota," Claire recounts. "People were asking me if I had this tractor or knew of someone who did."

In 1976, Claire and his friend Loren Larson learned that the Ertl Company was selling off hundreds of obsolete farm toys for two dollars apiece, regardless of what the toy was. Scheibe and Larson looked through the tractors, swathers, spreaders, combines, and chuck wagons and decided to buy more than a hundred toys. With so many toys in his inventory, Scheibe started sending a single-page typewritten letter to other collectors, a letter that became the nucleus for *Toy Farmer* magazine.

Another event spurred the actual startup of the magazine. Morgan Williams, director of the Farmers Home Administration in Kansas, was on his way to a meeting in Bismarck, North Dakota, when he stopped by Scheibe's farm to talk toys. Williams showed Claire a trunkload of "pot metal" toys which, he said, were the next hot collectible.

"Someone like you could really make this thing go," Williams told Scheibe. "You are the person I think could do the job of telling the story about it and keeping people acquainted with possibly what's happening with farm toys."

Scheibe began scouring the country, visiting farm implement dealerships, hardware stores, and variety stores in his search for old toys. "It was interesting that in those days the merchants and dealers were more than happy to give you a generous discount if you bought all of their old inventory," he notes.

In late 1977, some of Scheibe's collector friends urged him to start publishing a newsletter about farm toy collecting. After much consideration, Claire and Cathy announced that they would begin publishing in January 1978.

With no journalism, photography, graphics, or publishing experience, the Scheibes began publishing a black-and-white, six-page *Toy Farmer* for seventeen subscribers who had sent in their $7.50 for a one-year subscription. The Scheibes borrowed $500 from the bank to finance their modest publishing plans. They had many doubts about the venture. "The least amount of newsletters the printer would print was 250," Claire recalls. "I thought it would at least make a modest bonfire."

By June 1978, *Toy Farmer* had grown to more than 500 subscribers who had spread the word by mouth.

As *Toy Farmer* grew during the late 1970s and early 1980s, the Scheibes still farmed and operated a large custom combining operation. In 1981, while Claire was sitting in his combine service truck late at night trying to write the next editorial, he realized he either had to stay in farming full time or go into publishing full time. He said to himself, "This is ridiculous. I've got to make up my mind." He sold the custom combining business and his farmland, other than the land where his farmstead is located, and devoted all of his effort to the magazine, farm toy shows, and toy manufacturing.

"It was a big step for us to decide, based on 6,000 subscribers, to make it a full-time business," says Cathy Scheibe. "It meant things like selling the farm." That was sixteen years ago, and *Toy Farmer* has been growing ever since.

In January 1986, the newsletter format gave way to a slick magazine format that has grown to nearly a hundred pages per month. The initial subscription list of 17 collectors has grown to more than 29,000 subscribers around the world.

"Most people collect because of nostalgia," Claire says. "They have a farm background, or farm ties. They had a toy just like that when they were a kid, or their farm machinery looked like that. You can take a farm toy and remember a time with your grandfather or father. It brings back good memories." After finding that link to the past, they're hooked; Scheibe himself has 600 toys.

Nowadays, *Toy Farmer*, along with its sister publication, *Toy Trucker & Contractor*, is produced in a special office building constructed on the Scheibe's farmstead. The publishing business is represented on its own Internet page. The Scheibes also had a hand in starting the National Farm Toy Museum in Dyersville, Iowa. In addition, *Toy Farmer* produces a commemorative farm toy for the National Farm Toy Show each November when 20,000 people descend on the small town for a three-day show where thousands of farm toys are sold and traded.

Today, little happens in the farm toy world that does not in some way have the imprint of Claire Scheibe and *Toy Farmer*.

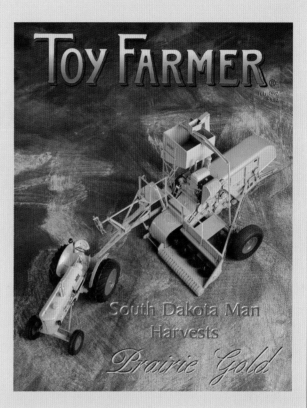

Toy Farmer magazine

Ertl Case 800
This 1/16 Case 800 Case-O-Matic tractor was built in 1990 by Ertl for Toy Farmer *magazine for the thirteenth annual National Farm Toy Show held annually in Dyersville, Iowa.*

Ertl International Harvester 1026

Above: *Special, limited-edition tractors are built for a variety of farm toy shows, like this 1/16 International Harvester 1026 Hydro tractor, which was made by Ertl for the 1997 Summer Farm Toy Show held annually in Dyersville, Iowa.*

Minneapolis-Moline collectors

Right, top: *Minneapolis-Moline collectors Dennis, left, and Dwight Gerszewski of Manvel, North Dakota, show the comparison between the toys and the real McCoy. (Photograph by Bill Vossler)*

John Deere collector

Right, bottom: *John Deere collector Irvin Kamrud of Bottineau, North Dakota, has all his farm toys on shelves in a special room in his house. (Photograph by Bill Vossler)*

Ertl Farmall Regular

Facing page: *This stunning 1/16 Farmall Regular is a prime example of the detail and quality of Ertl's Precision Series tractors.*

Chapter 2

The Die Is Cast: Farm Toy Materials

Through the ages, farm toys have been made out of just about every type of material one can imagine. To make one's own farm toys, anything and everything was a possible material, but commercially made farm toys have primarily been produced in cast iron, die-cast steel, rubber, and plastic, as well as out of various other materials. The type of material that a farm toy is made of can determine how long it lasts and how desirable it is to collectors today, both of which affect the prices of farm toys.

Wood

Stratford, South Dakota, farm toy collector Lloyd Jark's eyes light up when he talks about the first toy tractors he constructed as a kid during the Great Depression: "We made our toys out of blocks of wood, with wheels made of spools that used to have thread on them. We used a spoon for a plow." To make a tractor cab, Jark drove a nail through two blocks of wood. "A Mason jar lid might work for a wheel, too. You drove your nail through it and then saw if it turned. We thought it was great. To make our drag, we drove shingle nails through a board, and to pull it, we used little pieces of string attached to the tractor. We also made our own gas station. We had a lot of fun. We used a lot of imagination in those days. We did it all by hand. Too bad we didn't keep that stuff."

Richard Birklid of rural Nome, North Dakota, also made his own toys, including swathers, binders, and plows "out of wood and whatever I could find around the place." He made a plow out of old used table spoons. "I had six or eight of them as plow bottoms. We cleared out bare dirt between rows of trees, and we'd have that for the fields. We'd play farming. We'd plow and do everything. I was the only boy, but I had two sisters who were younger. Mostly I'd play by myself, but sometimes I'd let the girls help me play, and sometimes I wouldn't," he laughs.

The only mass-produced wooden farm toy made by a major farm toy manufacturer was a wagon with a wood flare-box on cast-iron gear sold by Arcade in 1940.

Several small toy makers used wood for their products through the years. Don Gross, a collector and farm toy show organizer from Albert Lea, Minnesota, has a wood threshing machine. "When I saw [it], I figured, 'Good grief, I've never seen anything like that before.' It really does look like a threshing machine, even though it was made of ordinary scrap wood and tin. It's very complete and very realistic." Unfortunately, the maker and vintage of this rare wooden thresher remains a mystery.

The wooden 1/16 Peter-Mar toy tractors were made in the 1940s by Peter Products Manufacturing of Muscatine, Iowa. Strombecker Plastic Company of Rock Island, Illinois, also made several brands of wagons in wood to pull behind the Peter-Mar tractors, according to Dick Sonnek, farm toy collector, historian, and author of the annual *Dick's Farm Toy Price Guide and Check List*.

Farm toy scratchbuilder Tom Dolan of Kaukauna, Wisconsin, made quite a few different wooden farm toys, such as chopper boxes and silage blowers. Collector and farm toy dealer Rick Campbell of Apple River, Illinois, noted that Dolan made a pull-type Gehl, Hesston, and other makes of choppers with corn-type and haylage heads.

Other wood farm toys were made by Marvin Kruse, who made seven 1/10 Allis-Chalmers models from 1979 through 1983, including an Allis-Chalmers WC row-crop on rubber in 1981 and an Allis-Chalmers 6/12 on steel wheels with a wide front end in 1983. He also made 1/10 models of Case C and L tractors in 1981 and 1982, respectively, both with wide front ends and steel wheels.

Dan Gubbels also made wooden farm toys, including more than two dozen tractors, many of them Allis-Chalmers, such as a 1/12 WD-45 LPG model in 1980 with a wide front end and a 1/12 WC row-crop on rubber wheels in both styled and unstyled versions in 1980.

Scratchbuilder Derwin Jensen of Hutchinson, Minnesota, regularly makes all-wood tractors and farm implements, among other items. Jensen got his start in

Product Miniature Farmall M
Previous page: *Product Miniature manufactured this plastic Farmall M in 1950 with a narrow front end. Several different variations were made of this same tractor: Some of the PM Farmall Ms were white with red wheels, whereas a rare gold variation is worth $1,200 in excellent condition in the 1990s. Collection: State Historical Society of Wisconsin.*

Wooden International Harvester

A fine handmade example of an International Harvester 86 series tractor with a mixer mill. Most volume-produced farm toys were not made of wood.

Olivers made from different materials

Three 1935 Model 70 Oliver tractors: from left to right, a die-cast replica on steel wheels; homemade wooden model; die-cast toy on rubber wheels. Collection: Dennis Gerszewski.

Sears Marx tractor advertisement

This tin-toy farm tractor set was listed in the 1929 Sears Roebuck catalog as "Our biggest seller in a mechanical toy and one of our best values": the price was a mere one dollar. The set was probably made by Marx as it was crafted of tin with lithographed details and a windup clockwork motor. As the catalog text brayed, "Just imagine the fun the kiddies will have hitching the different pieces behind the tractor to do the different jobs around your farm, just like Dad does with his big tractor." The set contained a tractor with a male driver, a four-wheel wagon, two-wheel rake, and disc harrow.

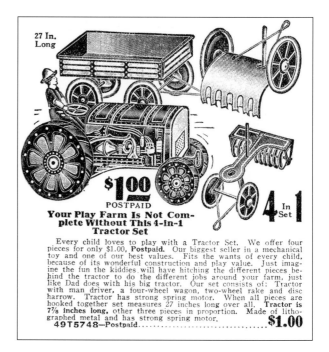

1991 when he made a Ford Model T roadster for his sister. Someone saw it and asked Derwin if he would make a wooden John Deere Model A tractor, and Jensen's business spiraled from there.

At first, Jensen built his tractors primarily out of pine. "Which was fine," Jensen said, "but as I got more familiar with other woods, I decided some of them just felt better, or looked better." He now uses woods such as black walnut for seat cushions, batteries, steering wheels, and "sometimes an exhaust pipe." Hard maple is used for the hood, radiator, and frame. "The tires are made of pine, mainly because it takes quite a bit of wood for the tires, and pine is more plentiful than all the different kinds of wood." For other toys, such as semi-trucks, Jensen uses just about every kind of wood imaginable from sources around the globe.

Tin

The manufacture of tin toys started in the United States and flowered from the mid-1800s through the 1930s. The "tin" was actually sheet steel coated with a thin layer of tin; the tin was used as a coating because it was rust resistant. The steel was blanked out from sheets with a die, curved or shaped, and then fastened together with either solder or bent-over tabs. Early tin toys typically had details painted on by freehand; later tin toys were stenciled.

While tin was used to make a wide variety of classic toys, it was not often used to make farm toys. Some

historians believe this is because the tin was not durable enough to withstand farmyard play. Others believe that the tin did not lend itself to getting the actual lines and details of a toy tractor; whenever tin was used for farm toys, the tractors had a squared-off appearance that did not represent the real machine.

Nevertheless, a small number of farm toys were made of tin. The Louis Marx & Company of New York City was the most famous of tin toy makers, and it made the most tin farm toys. Among its line was an 8-inch-long (200-mm) "American Tractor" wind-up toy in 1926; a Co-Op tin friction combine that was 6 inches long (150 mm); a farm tractor and implement set in 1948 that consisted of a tin wind-up tractor with a mower, hayrake, and three-gang plow; and the "Sparkling Tractor" of the 1950s. Sears Roebuck offered a variety of tin farm toys, from animals to tractors, in its catalogs into the 1930s; many of these were produced by Marx.

Kingsbury made a tin "Kingsbury" tractor and cart with an iron driver and white rubber wheels in the 1930s.

A few implements were constructed of tin, most of them produced by Carter in 1950. Carter's tin implements include the rare orange 1/16 Allis-Chalmers flare-box wagon; an orange 1/16 Case grain flare-box with rubber wheels; a 1/16 Case two-bottom pull-type plow; a red 1/16 Minneapolis-Moline four-gang disc plow.

The Slik-Toy Company of Lansing, Iowa, made a 1/40 Oliver farm set out of tin in 1950.

Several tin farm implements were made by an unknown manufacturer in 1950: the scarce Allis-Chalmers single-gang disc of two variations, along with companion pieces of a rare orange two-section drag harrow, and a scarce orange two-bottom plow, both Allis-Chalmers.

The De Laval Cream Separator Company made cows, calves, and a cream separator of tin.

Cast Iron

During the 1870s, approximately sixteen years before the first commercially produced farm toy was made, toy manufacturers began to explore the possibilities of cast iron. At the time, tin toys were at the peak of their popularity, but tin was not truly durable enough for constructing long-lasting toys; cast iron was durable and also less expensive.

Cast-iron toys were made by pouring molten iron into the cavity of a sand mold and letting gravity settle it. The later die-cast toys, on the other hand, used an actual metal mold in the form of the toy, and molten metal—initially steel—was forced under pressure into the mold and allowed to harden. Cast-iron molds can only make a single toy; die-cast molds can be used over again to mass produce toys in high volume.

Many early commercial farm toys were made of cast iron, including those of Arcade, Vindex, Hubley, Kenton, and others. Cast-iron toys became so popular that they were made until the outbreak of World War II, when iron was needed for the war effort. Following the war, cast iron was eventually edged out by lighter-weight toys made of tin, steel, or plastic, which could be shipped for less cost—an important factor in controlling production margins.

Today, these vintage cast-iron farm toys bring premium prices. "Cast iron toys," David Longest wrote in the book *Toys, Antique & Collectible,* "are considered by some to be the 'Cadillac' area of toy collecting because of the high quality of the toys and the high prices they command at toy shows and auctions."

In the late 1990s, the 1/16 Vindex John Deere manure spreader can bring $3,000, whereas the Vindex John Deere pull-type combine of 1930 can garner up to $6,000. Hubley's 1938 8½-inch-long (212-mm) Fordson tractor with a loader can bring up to $1,800; 1/16 Arcade McCormick-Deering threshers with

moveable feeders can bring $1,200; and 1/16 McCormick-Deering 10/20 tractors made by Arcade may fetch $500 or more.

Farm toy collectors either love cast iron, or they hate it, because the toys are expensive, and many were crudely made.

Lead

Only one American farm toy was cast from lead, a 1/32 John Deere Model D tractor made in 1930 by the Kansas Toy Novelty Company of Clifton, Kansas. Unfortunately, the Kansas Deere D has poor detail.

Some Fun Ho! farm toys from New Zealand were made of lead. Fun Ho! made toy tractors from 1935 to 1960, including a Fordson F, Massey-Harris 44, and Oliver 70 Orchard.

Pressed Steel

The process for making pressed-steel toys is similar to that for crafting tin toys. Pressed-steel toys are stamped out of steel that is rolled flat. Huge stamping presses cut out the parts, and other stamping tools down the line bend and form it into the correct shape.

Most farm toys made in pressed steel were implements, and most of these were Tru-Scale toys crafted by Joe Carter from 1952 through 1972. Some of these Tru-Scale toys included 1/16 wagons, or farm sets, like the Farmall M tractor with disc, two-bottom plow, and two-wheel trailer. Carter also made a wide variety of pressed-steel toys under the Carter name, including John Deere combines, balers, and corn pickers.

Lincoln Specialties of Canada made a Cockshutt wagon barge in 1950. Slik made several pressed-steel items, including a Minneapolis-Moline wagon in 1950. Hubley made pressed-steel plows in 1956 and Ford plows, among other farm toys.

The Standi company of St. Paul, Minnesota, made a Gehl pressed-steel mixer-grinder in 1982. Ertl made a variety of pressed-steel farm toys, including a 1/16 Case gravity wagon in 1986. Scratchbuilder Wayne Eisele of Waterloo, Iowa, made a pressed-steel loader.

Few tractors were made in pressed steel. One was a John Deere Dain tractor fabricated by Hansen in 1982.

The Eska Company made many pedal tractors of pressed steel, as well as two-wheel trailers. BMC made pedal tractors in pressed steel.

Kenton Fordson F

Above: *The Kenton Hardware Company of Kenton, Ohio, made this Fordson F cast-iron farm toy with an air cleaner cast in behind the engine. Collection: State Historical Society of Wisconsin.*

Kansas Toy John Deere D

Left: *The Kansas Toy Novelty Company of Clifton, Kansas, made this 1/32 John Deere Model D tractor from cast lead in the 1930s. Because it shows such poor detail, it is not a highly sought-after farm toy, but it is one of the few lead farm toys produced in the United States. Collection: Eldon Trumm.*

Pressed-steel farm toys appeal to collectors for a variety of reasons, from their rarity to their vintage. Collector Jasper Bond of St. Cloud, Minnesota, says he buys pressed-steel toys for reasons different from most collectors: "As an artist, I could imagine how they looked when you unfolded them and flattened them out, the ones that were made out of one piece of steel. That intrigued me."

Sand-Cast Aluminum

Sand-cast aluminum (SCA) toys are made much like cast-iron toys. Molten aluminum is poured into the cavity of a special sand mold, which can be used only once.

SCA farm toys include Slik's 1/16 Oliver toy tractors from the late 1940s to the early 1960s. These include a 1/16 Oliver 77 and Oliver 880, and 1/32 Oliver 880.

Many collector models have been made of SCA, such as the Oliver 880 made by custom-builder Lyle Dingman of Spencer, Iowa; the Steiger III Cougar from Valley Patterns of Fargo, North Dakota; the Twin City tractors by custom-builder Bob Gray of Eldora, Iowa; and the 1/8 tractors from Scale Models of Dyersville, Iowa, such as the Farmall M and Deere B.

Spun-Cast

Spun-cast toys are made from metals with low melting points, such as pewter, zinc, aluminum, or lead. Molten metal is poured into the center of a rapidly rotating set of rubber molds. The metal is flung outward into the mold cavity by centrifugal force, cooling enough in the process so the rubber of the mold is not burned, and filling all the nooks and crannies of the mold.

Spun-cast toys have been manufactured mainly by the Spec-Cast Company of Dyersville, Iowa, such as a 1/43 scale Allis-Chalmers RC tractor in 1994. Paul Stephan's Stephan Manufacturing of Beloit, Wisconsin, also crafted a 1/16 John Deere 820 in 1991.

American Precision Allis-Chalmers C
This 1/16 Allis-Chalmers C was made by American Precision Products from sand-cast aluminum in 1948. The rubber tires were produced by Firestone, maker of rubber tires for actual tractors. Collection: State Historical Society of Wisconsin.

43

Auburn rubber tractors

Above: *These are two of the many color variations of rubber tractors made by the Auburn Rubber Company of Auburn, Indiana. The tractor is a replica of a John Deere, although the tractor comes in at least seven different colors.*

Standi John Deere 530

Only 450 of these wide-front 1/16 John Deere 530 tractors were built by the Standi firm of St. Paul, Minnesota. These toys were made of plastic in 1986, but do not carry much value today, selling for about forty-five dollars each. Only 250 of the same model with narrow front ends were made at the same time, and their value is the same.

7-PC. RUBBER TRACTOR, ANIMAL SET

Here's the first **all rubber** tractor with rubber wheels. Length, 4¼ in.; plus, a horse 3¾ in. long; colt 2¼ in. long. Cow, dog, sheep in proportion. 11-in. fence with opening gate. Ideal for little tots, all pieces molded from soft solid rubber. **Unbreakable, Sanitary, Life-like, Washable.**

49 F 6413—Shipping weight, 1 lb. 8 oz.... **49c**

Sears rubber tractor advertisement
In 1937, Sears Roebuck offered this seven-piece rubber tractor and animal set for forty-nine cents. The catalog asserted that this tractor was "the first all rubber tractor with rubber wheels." The set included a horse, cow, dog, and sheep. The toys were promised to be "Unbreakable, Sanitary, Life-like, Washable."

Most spun-cast zinc toys today are made by Spec-Cast. These include the company's collector model 1/16 and 1/43 Allis-Chalmers D-14.

Other well-known spun-cast zinc toys are those made by custom-builder Gilson Rieke of Ruthven, Iowa, including his collector model Allis-Chalmers G. Lyle Dingman has also made some spun-cast zinc toys, like his Case DC in 1983.

Rubber

The major manufacturer of rubber farm toys was the Auburn Rubber Company of Auburn, Indiana. Anyone who has spent time with toys has doubtless seen Auburn's rubber tractor replicas of the 1950s.

In the 1950s, Auburn abandoned rubber as its material of choice. The firm soon was producing vehicles made only of vinyl: Liquid plastic was forced into die-cast steel or resin molds to form the toys. Shortly thereafter, Auburn went out of business.

Auburn made rubber replicas of Oliver, John Deere, International Harvester, Allis-Chalmers, and other tractors. Among the firm's toys were a red-and-silver Allis-Chalmers tractor and two Minneapolis-Moline Z tractors made starting in 1950.

One of Auburn's subsidiary brands was Arcor of Connellsville, Pennsylvania, which made several rubber tractors, such as its yellow-and-red Minneapolis-Moline R tractors in 1940 and 1946.

Plastic

As plastic came of age after World War II, companies began to use it for toys, as it was lighter and less expensive to make and ship than iron or tin. Unfortunately, many of the firms thought the early plastic would be more durable than it was.

In 1950, Product Miniature (PM) of Milwaukee, Wisconsin, made several plastic 1/16 farm toys, including a rare pair of Allis-Chalmers WD tractors, one with a flare-box wagon, the other with a wagon and an Allis-Chalmers HD-5 crawler with a Baker blade. The A-C WD tractor is a "fragile model," according to Dick Sonnek in *Dick's Farm Toy Price Guide and Check List*, and he notes that the toy breaks easily and, hence, is difficult to find in pristine condition. The firm also produced a pair of A-C wagons, one a rare flare-box, the other a barge-box. In addition, PM made a Farmall M in 1950 in different variations; a plastic IH wagon in 1950; a 1/12 Ford 8N tractor in 1952; 1/12 Ford NAA and Ford 600 tractors in 1953; a Ford 900 row-crop in 1954; and others.

Ertl's plastic toys included a 1/16 barge-type IH wagon kit in 1972; a 1/25 IH 1466 kit in 1974; an IH 1086 radio control in 1980; a 1/32 Ford TW-20 radio-controlled tractor in 1982; a Ford FW60 in 1986 for *Toy Farmer* magazine of LaMoure, North Dakota; a battery-powered 1/32 Case 5120 in 1990; and many more.

There were numerous other plastic tractors from a variety of makers from the 1950s to the 1990s, listed here in alphabetical order. Afinson, ATMA, Design Fabricators (DF), Saunders & Swader (SS), and Reuhl all made 1/16 Farmall Cubs in 1950. Airfix of England released a 1/20 Ferguson TE-30 kit in 1950. Auburn switched from rubber to vinyl toys in the 1950s and made a 1/16 red-and-silver Allis-Chalmers tractor in 1950, and also made other plastic models. C&M, the company run by Coleman and Mary Wheatley of Springfield, Illinois, made a Cockshutt 550 in 1990.

Johan of Detroit, Michigan, produced Case 800 tractors in 1956 and 1957. Kemp made plastic tractors, including a Canadian Farmall M in 1950, so named because it was made for Canadian implement dealers and farmers; two Cockshutt 30s in 1954; and implements, as well as a red Cockshutt barge wagon. Lakone-Classic of Aurora, Illinois, created an International C in 1950, and IH 200 and 230 tractors in the mid-1950s. Model Products Corporation (MPC) of Milwaukee, Wisconsin, made a 1/12 Ford 8N in 1952. Monarch Plastics produced a 1/16 Case manure spreader in 1950, Case farm set in 1950, and Case SC tractors in 1950 and 1951, one without fenders, the second with. Strombecker made two styles of the Allis-Chalmers D-14 tractor in 1957. TM made a Ferguson mounted plow in 1955 and a gray 1/12 Ferguson TO-30 tractor.

Other manufacturers of plastic farm toys included Britains, Florida Classic Farm Toys, France, Lipkin, Marbil, Scale Models, Standi, and Trumm.

Custom-builder Weldon Yoder of New Paris, Indiana, has made many tractors in plastic, including two Case 700s in 1986 and 1991; an Allis-Chalmers D-15 tractor in 1988; and three Case 400 tractors in 1991.

Collectors are often divided concerning plastic toys, or the use of plastic on die-cast models. Collector Joe Large of Owaneco, Illinois, isn't a fan of plastic. He doesn't like the Ertl 1280 combine with the plastic reel, for instance. "I liked the old one with the metal reel," he said. "The same way with the tractor: Instead of putting plastic wheels on, they should put metal wheels on."

The farm toys most often made of plastic were International Harvester replicas; John Deere miniatures were the least often fabricated of plastic.

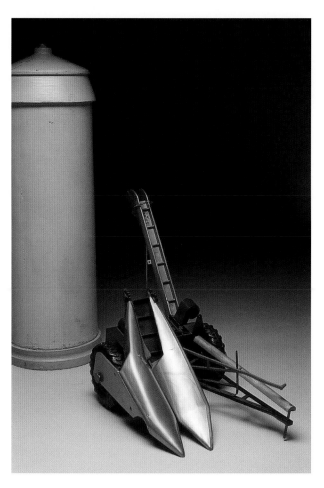

Topping New Idea corn picker
This plastic 1/16 New Idea corn picker was manufactured by Topping Models in 1950. It is worth $300 in the 1990s.

Die-Cast Steel

Die-cast steel is the modern method of choice for making farm toys. Die-cast steel farm toys are made by forcing molten steel under pressure into the cavity of a metal mold (as opposed to molds made of sand as with cast-iron and sand-cast aluminum), and allowed to harden. This modern high-tech method allows toy manufacturers to mass produce high volumes of toys from a single mold.

Die-cast steel farm toys range from Ertl's latest Allis-Chalmers D-17 tractor to Scale Model's White 4-270 four-wheel-drive tractor, and all kinds of tractors and implements in between.

Brass

Scale Models has made several brass farm toys, including Massey-Ferguson 135 and 1100 tractors. Custom- and scratch-makers will employ brass as one of the materials in making their tractors as well.

Cardboard

Cardboard was used only for making farm sets, such as the Ertl 1/64 equipped farmyard or equipped IH dealership, both made in 1981.

Korloy

The only toys made in any number of this aluminum-lead alloy were made by custom-builder Bob Gray, such as his Buffalo-Pitts 40/70 steam engine from 1974, or his 1/12 Farmall F-30 collector model in 1969.

Several other builders and companies experimented with korloy farm toys, including Pioneers of Power's 1/12 Ford tractor of 1978 with a wide front end on steel wheels that was a replica of the Arcade Ford 2N.

Charles Souhrada made a korloy 1/16 Fordson F toy in 1975 in American and English versions, with a driver, wide front end, and fenders.

Spec-Cast John Deere series
Pewter is the material of choice for these 1/43 John Deere machines from the 1990s. The series is made by the Spec-Cast Company of Dyersville, Iowa. The tractors include (clockwise from top): a John Deere truck, Waterloo Boy, John Deere AR, John Deere 730, and a Froehlich tractor, thought to be the first gas tractor ever invented. This pewter Froehlich replica was made for the 1993 Parts Expo, a dealer meeting in Nashville, Tennessee. Collection: Eldon Trumm.

Pewter

Spec-Cast is the only manufacturer that makes pewter toys, including the firm's collector model 100th anniversary IH thresher, John Deere Froehlich tractor, and Overtime tractor. Pewter farm toys are almost always made in 1/43 scale.

Resin

Custom-builder Roger Mohr of Vail, Iowa, has made several resin farm toys, like his Minneapolis-Moline 705 and 706 tractors.

Scratchbuilder Jeff Ceroll of Harrisburg, South Dakota, has also made some resin farm toys, such as his Twin City Model J tractor.

Gary Anderson made a 1/16 Oliver 88 row-crop with wide front end in 1984.

Lincoln Specialties John Deere A
Lincoln Specialties of Canada made this 1/16 John Deere A during the 1950s. The green paint used is lighter than on other Deere tractors, as the color has faded with age. Collection: Eldon Trumm.

Ertl Case 1170 Agri King

This gold-plated 1/16 Case 1170 Agri King was made by Ertl for the 1996 National Farm Toy Show. Ertl built 1,400 of these Cases, two of which were plated with gold.

Grown men don't collect little farm toys.

For many years that was the sentiment, even among farm toy people. Louis Hertz wrote in the book *The Toy Collector* that many men would like to collect actual old wagons, fire engines, and machinery of all sorts. "A few do, to their benefit and that of the world at large," Hertz states, "but for most it is obviously impractical for a variety of reasons, of which lack of available space alone is usually sufficient to preclude them from carrying out such inclinations. However, these things can be collected and are widely collected as reflected in contemporary toys."

And yet in the farm toy field, having those little tractors and implements seemed somehow unmanly—especially for big, burly farmers. So for years people would go to their local farm implement dealer and buy toys "for my children," or "for my grandchildren."

But bit by bit, these closet collectors discovered each other, usually by accident. Collector Joe Male of Millington, Michigan, says he attends more than fifty toy shows a year, "and as I'm watching the crowd go by, I'll see two men stop and start talking. 'Wow, what are you doing here?' 'I collect toys.' 'I never knew that!' These are neighbors who have known each other for years, or people who have worked together, and they both collect toys, but they never knew that the other one collected. But at a farm toy show, they're safe. I think there are still quite a few closet collectors who collect toys, or want to collect toys, but they don't advertise it because they're still afraid that they'll be judged that they're still children."

Collector Don Woehl of Wishek, North Dakota, found in his toolshed a 1/16 Oliver 1850 toy tractor that had belonged to his son. He had a friend, Don Holzer, restore it, and after that, he was hooked on collecting and fixing up his own toys. Woehl did this for a year until he had a whole slug of them hidden away in his tool shed. "Then one day I bought a long glass showcase and put it in our basement," he says. "I put my toys in it, and suddenly my wife knew about the toys. I had been scared that she would be mad at me."

Instead, his wife, Gardenia, was supportive. "Although if he ever starts going 'brr-brr-brr' and driving them, I don't know what I'll do," she laughs.

But it isn't just the opinions of others that farm toy people fear—sometimes it's their own opinion. One day, Ronald Eliason of Buxton, North Dakota, saw the toy collection belonging to Dave Thomas of Hillsboro, North Dakota. "When I saw his, I knew that was what I wanted to do. When I saw what he had, and found out what other people had in their collections, then I began to be outspoken about having a toy collection. I had always thought tractor collecting was for kids and not grownups."

Sometimes that stigma got people into trouble. David Steele of Jamestown, North Dakota, remembers that his late father-in-law, Ben Sundstrom, would disappear for a few days from time to time. "He never clued us in to where he had gone," Steele remembers, and people wondered what he had been doing.

Then Steele discovered the secret: Sundstrom was a farm toy collector. "He didn't tell anyone at first. He didn't want people to think he was losing it," says Steele. However, instead of thinking Sundstrom was "losing it," Steele was intrigued. "I had gotten some toys for my boy when he was born in 1982. I thought 'He'll like them when he gets older.'" But once he discovered his father-in-law's passion, Steele went with him to a toy show in the Grand Forks area. "On the way home I was thinking of all the toys I had had when I was a kid." A glimmer of hope had sprung up in Steele's breast. He knew his old toys were still in super condition, because

Advance-Rumely OilPull collector
Above: *John Peternell of Albany, Minnesota, is one of the many middle-aged collectors. He has all of the different varieties of real Advance-Rumely OilPull tractors made, so it was natural that he might have a few of the toys, too, like this 1919 16/30 Advance-Rumely OilPull in 1/16 scale. (Photograph by Bill Vossler)*

as a kid he'd been such a perfectionist that he had washed off all his farm toys every time he was finished playing with them. "That used to drive everybody crazy. But after the Grand Forks show, I went home to try to find my old tractors and trucks and Tonkas." His hopes were dashed: His mother had given them away to neighbor kids. But at least he had rediscovered farm toys.

During the mid-1980s, farm toy shows proliferated across the heartland of the United States and Canada, and the network of collectors made contact with each other. Also, *Toy Farmer* magazine made its influence felt, uniting disparate collectors and adding information about the field, as well as establishing its annual National Farm Toy Show held in Dyersville, Iowa. Publisher Claire Scheibe said in 1986, "Collectors are coming out of the closet now. A grown person can collect farm toys, just like collecting rocks or stamps or coins."

Not all the negative residue toward farm toy collectors has disappeared today, however, as Barry Hall of Mulberry, Florida, knows well. Sometimes, other people's perspectives merely need to be altered by using the right examples. In his case, Hall says his father used to give him a bad time about collecting farm toys, asking when he was going to grow up. "So one time I asked him how much he'd spent on his hobby that particular year—he'd gotten new golf clubs—and he said $2,000. I asked him how much he'd made, and he said nothing. Well, I told him I'd spent about the same amount on my hobby, but I'd sold about $4,000 worth of toys, plus the toys I'm keeping are increasing in value, so at least my hobby was making me some money." Since then, Hall says, his father always tells people to be sure to see his son's farm toy show in March in Mulberry.

Why have so many people come out of the closet in terms of farm toys? First, because it does not carry the stigma it used to. Second, the toys recreate the nostalgia of childhood. "Perhaps," Hertz wrote in *The Toy Collector*, "they recapture the past better than the actual objects which they emulate, for toys have ever been the windows through which children first see and realize the full-sized world, and toys mold the viewpoints and ideals that are later carried into adult life."

As Lyle Hovland of Rothsay, Minnesota, says, "When I was sixteen or seventeen years old, I was collecting, but I wasn't going to let any of my peers know I was playing with toys, or that I liked toys."

But in about 1980, Hovland saw a story on Dick Sonnek's collection in the *Farm Journal*, and he read about *Toy Farmer* magazine. "In the magazine was a list of toy shows. I went to my first one in Des Moines, Iowa. I was still a closet collector. When I bought the large tractor for my farm, I always bought the small one too.

"Let me tell you, it was exciting to find out there were other collectors out there. I was so excited after that show that I didn't sleep that night, discovering there were all kinds of toys there, most of which I had never seen or heard of, and other collectors as well."

Toy farmer
A smiling Loren Stier of Belle Plaine, Minnesota, shows off a few of his toys in his private farm toy museum. (Photograph by Bill Vossler)

Chapter 3

Tractors in Miniature: Toy Sizes and Scales

Starting in the 1920s, commercially built farm toys were made in 1/16 scale of the real machines. This meant that the toys were one-sixteenth the size of the real McCoy: 1 inch (25 mm) of the replica equaled 16 inches (400 mm) of the real machine. But why 1/16 scale was chosen is open to debate among toy historians and collectors.

The trend to 1/16 scale took off with the 1/16 Vindex toys of the 1930s, and other farm toy manufacturers followed the leader. Other collectors believe 1/16 was chosen because it was substantial enough for kids to play with in the sandbox. Still others claim it is the size most easily held in the hand. Whatever the reasons might be, farm toys for many years were traditionally made in 1/16 scale.

Jim Willey is Farm Toy Product Manager at the Ertl Company in Dyersville, Iowa, which manufactures many farm toys in different sizes. Willey says there is no rule concerning toy sizes. "My understanding, as I've been told over the years by different collectors and people involved in the hobby, is that the way toys were made in the early days was less about the scale of the toy—a tractor 1/16 or 1/64 the size of the real machine, for example—but rather the physical size the manufacturer wanted the toy to be. "Toy makers wanted their products to be "easily held in a child's hand," which translated into a size of about 10 inches long and 4 inches high (250x100 mm).

While the 1/16 scale is often quoted as a vintage or modern farm toy's size, many early toy models were not actually 1/16, but just slightly smaller. Willey explains: "When the sizing became a more exact science, builders made a size to agree with what had been done previously." So, as early farm toys were made at just less than 1/16 scale, modern toys followed the same "rule."

Regardless of the actual scale, the parts of the toy also had to be proportionally accurate. Everything about the toy—tires, gear levers, and so on—was supposed to be correct in relation to its size on the real machine. Thus, the toy became an accurate model of the real machine, no matter in which scale it was done.

Some collectors, such as Ken Updike of Evanston,

Wisconsin, do not think that all of today's high-quality farm toys are proportionately correct. "There are so many toys out there that are not anatomically correct. They're not truly to scale if you really measure them. A lot of times they change some of the features on them to make them look right, like adding front weights, or making the exhaust bigger to look right. They're close, but not always accurate. Tires are close but they don't ever really match."

Still, 1/16 has become the standard. Collector John Kayser of Dell Rapids, South Dakota, says he has always liked the 1/16 size because of the detail. "The 1/16 is something you can play with. I don't get down on my hands and knees and purr like a motor any more, but I do like to hook up an implement to a tractor and sit and look at it."

Other Scales and Sizes

Farm toys come in other scales as well. Some include 1/12, 1/32, 1/43, and 1/64, says Gary Becker, Senior Director of Marketing for Farm Toys at the Ertl Company. The 1/50 scale has become popular for construction equipment toys, and the new, large-size 1/8 scale tractors created by Scale Models allows for even more detail.

But why and how were these sizes chosen? Why not 1/10, or 3/10, in keeping with the accepted American decimal system? Each of the current scales has a story of its own.

1/64 Scale: The Miniature Replica

Willey of Ertl explains the appeal of the small 1/64 scale: "The 1/64 has been very successful because of two factors: its relative size to other accepted toys in the marketplace; and that it was a derivative, or a multiple of the 1/16 scale." The 1/64 scale is four times smaller than the standard 1/16 scale.

In a more practical vein, the 1/64 models worked "because they're easily held by small hands," Willey said. "Plus both collectors and kids could fit more of them on the shelf compared to the 1/16, they weren't as cumbersome to play with, and you could easily take them along to grandma's. That's why the small toys

Scales of John Deere tractors
Previous page: *These John Deere tractors effectively show the different scales of farm tractors made. Clockwise from top left: the largest scale, a 1/8 John Deere B; 1/16 John Deere 4450; 1/32 John Deere 3140; 1/64 John Deere 50 series; and 1/43 John Deere 4020.*

Ertl Farmall 560
Ertl manufactured this 1/16 Farmall 560 during the 1960s. Collection: State Historical Society of Wisconsin.

became popular."

Collector Jasper Bond of St. Cloud, Minnesota, was one of the converts to 1/64. He says the small toys remind him of his childhood. "My father was a career army man, so we moved around a lot. I went to first grade in Alaska, third in Texas, fifth in Missouri, seventh in Kansas—eight schools in all—and all of high school in Illinois. So whatever I collected couldn't be big, because we moved so much. That was why I collected 1/64 scale farm toys."

But just because the tractors are small doesn't mean they can't be valuable. Collector Jerry Adams of Lakeland, Florida, says some of the 1/64 tractors he has are valuable right now. "Especially the John Deere with a hook on the hitch instead of a hole in the hitch. They only made so many of them. You see them at swap meets—a little dinky tractor like that going for $150. I have the whole series; little boxes that came in one big box for like $7.98 for the whole series. And now

they are always tight; people are always looking for them."

The 1/64 scale is ideal for creating farm country sets. Willey says it would be expensive and impractical to build farm country buildings in 1/16 scale, simply due to their potential size. "But you can do it very satisfactorily in the 1/64 scale. So it becomes a very agreeable play scale to make a whole farm, instead of maybe just one tractor out in the field."

Like many collectors who start in 1/16 and build a large collection, Al Van Kley of Ankeny, Iowa, ran out of room for his 1/16 scale toys. "So I quit collecting the 1/16, except for an occasional red tractor or four-wheel-drive tractor, and switched to 1/64. Of course, I keep a few John Deere to keep my wife, Cathy, happy," he smiles. "From there, it didn't take me long to go totally to 1/64 scale toys. The cost is much more reasonable for most 1/64 scale toys."

Becker of Ertl adds that detail and price are other

factors in 1/64 scale farm toys. "A collector of 1/64 scale is generally going to expect a little less detail than a 1/16 scale collector." In addition, 1/64 coincides with the S gauge of model railroading, part of the consideration of why 1/64 became an established size, according to Willey.

When collector Michael Brasda of Poynette, Wisconsin, found out about 1/64 scale tractors, he bought more than thirty of them immediately. "I thought I had all of them," he laughs. Now he's at 550 and counting.

1/32 Scale: Driven by European Collectors

"What really drove the 1/32 size," says Willey, "is the European toy market. The demand from the European market for good replicas became a primary driver for our production of them." He adds that the European market doesn't have much in the 1/16 scale, "and they're relatively minor in anything 1/64. If you go to most any European country, 1/32 scale is the scale,

and we began producing them to address that market. It was also a multiple of the 1/16, halfway between the 1/16 and 1/64, and made sense from that aspect."

Willey says he can only speculate why Europe chose 1/32. "I would guess that where Mr. Ertl made his first units in the family furnace back in Dubuque in 1945, his counterpart in Europe did the same thing, only smaller. It's purely speculation, but it has to have its roots somewhere, and I'd guess it's that type of story. Each category tends to have its own history."

In a letter to the editor of *Toy Farmer* magazine in March 1997, collectors Steve and Karen Harris of Great Britain agreed that "1/32 scale is the sensible choice. This is something we in Europe have settled on for a long time and find that the combination of the size and detail that is achievable in a 1/32 model matches that of the larger, more unwieldy 1/16 models.

"Of course, the USA has a long tradition of toys, dating back to the early cast-iron toys to the more recent Ertl models, being in large, easy-to-play-with models that would both appeal to the youngster and

Tootsietoy farm truck
This tiny Tootsietoy farm truck, made by the Cosmo Toy and Novelty Company, measures just ¾ inch (2 cm) in length. Collection: State Historical Society of Wisconsin.

allow a reasonable amount of detail to be incorporated with the cruder patternmaking methods of those early days. The prototype machinery was considerably smaller back then. Also, the size of the family farmhouses allowed for the accumulation of large collections with room to store and display the models. Now the U.S.A. is following Europe with increasing property costs leading people to downsize their homes to realize capital or with modern homes and apartments leading to less room for model display and storage."

In only a couple of years, collector Vern Voll of rural Roseau, Minnesota, has completed a collection of 1/32 scale tractors, garnering all of them that have been made. He found many of them as he traveled for his job and bought toys all over the United States.

Voll was truly enamored with the 1/64 scale, "but I kept looking at the four-wheel-drive tractor in the 1/32 size—I love four-wheel drives—and I went after them. In a year and a half, I just about hit my goal to get them all." Versatile is the line he likes best. "They're a pretty tractor. In real life, it's the one I ride."

None of them were difficult for him to find, he says, because he got into collecting before they became scarce. He figures it would be pretty hard to get the entire collection he has right now, because there are just more collectors. Some U.S.-made 1/32 tractors include the plastic TW-20 Ford manufactured by Ertl in 1982 and the Ford friction 7710 made by Ertl in 1986.

1/50 Scale: For Construction Toys

The 1/50 scale has become popular for construction toys, primarily due to European toy makers. In the United States, Ertl produces 1/50 construction toys. Says Willey, "We produce, for instance, the Caterpillar in 1/50, and there's a lot of very high detail replica product, which mostly comes out of Germany and other European countries, in that 1/50 scale for construction. So there's kind of another collector branch which is interested in 1/50, which is why we produce our Caterpillar items in that scale."

1/43 Scale: A Hobbyist Size

The 1/43 scale was derived from collectors of other replica toys, such as automobiles. Willey explains: "The collector cars were there in that size before the tractors were, and because of the interest in those units,

we began producing the 1/43, basically because there was a demand for the farm equipment. Our production of them is a relatively minor-by-comparison group, but it's important to the people who collect it. That group is very much a collector group, and of course we know that the products that we put in that scale have to pay very close attention to detail. The 1/43 is more collector and less toy. Also, 1/43 is the old railroad scale."

Jasper Bond said when he saw the first 1/43 scale tractor, he bought it and put it on a railroad flatcar. "But it looked kind of funny on there alone, so I went out and bought three for each flatcar. Then at a train show I thought it would be fun to buy a bunch of flatcars, a green one for John Deere, an orange one for Allis, a red for IH, and have a farm train. That was my goal."

1/12 Scale: A Growing Interest

The 1/12 scale is a little-used size for farm toys that is slowly gaining in popularity. Ertl made several 1/12 scale toys in the 1970s, including Ford 7700, 8600, 9600, 9700, and other tractors. The rumor among collectors is that the Ford Motor Company required all early Ford toys to be made larger than other farm toys—1/12 instead of 1/16, for instance—which implied that its real tractors were more powerful than other real tractors. Whether true or not, it's a curious sidelight.

Scale Models makes 1/12 scale models, some of which are made from the old Hubley dies: Put the Hubley toy and the Scale Model 1/12 toys side by side, and the similarities are striking. One of the most valuable Hubleys recreated by Scale Models was a Farmall 806 made for the Ontario Show-Woodstock and cast from the old Hubley tooling. On the Farmall, one can see where "Hubley" was rubbed off and "Scale Models" substituted. Scale Models still makes some Hubley toys in 1/12 scale, including Ford 4000 and Ford 961 tractors.

Valley Patterns made 1/12 tractors, but had been out of business until restarting in 1997. Wayne Kyllo, whose father, Ron, originally started Valley Patterns, took over the company and started making 1/12 scale tractors again in 1997. Including variations, Valley Patterns has made about twenty different 1/12 scale toys and has recently been licensed to make John Deere products in 1/12.

Collector Ken Updike says he likes his 1/12 scale Steiger tractors built by Valley Patterns. "I like them because they are big and crude, and in real life tractors were big. I don't see where 1/64 really justifies real tractors, for me."

1/8 Scale: Bigger is Better

The newest farm toy size is the 1/8 scale. More collectors are looking for farm toys with greater detail, and the price of scratchbuilt and customized toys has grown out of bounds for many collectors. So, manufacturers have started making 1/8 scale models to allow even more detailed tractors.

Scale Models has made several 1/8 scale tractors: a Farmall M, Farmall 560, Farmall 806, John Deere B, John Deere 70, Ford 8N, Allis-Chalmers WD45, Oliver 1850, Massey-Harris 44, as well as a wagon and tandem disc harrow.

"1/8 isn't for everybody," says Updike, who handles all the toys at Carter & Gruenewald Implement of Brooklyn, Wisconsin. "We find that pricewise, the 1/8 scale aren't so different than the Precision Series tractors by Ertl, and we're finding that people will buy a 1/8 scale before a Precision, because the size justifies the price."

The disadvantage of 1/8 size, of course, is the room needed to house a growing collection of 1/8 toys. But for some people, that isn't a problem. The detail is more important.

One interesting insight into 1/8 models came from Jerry Adams of Lakeland, Florida, who worked as a general manager for a John Deere dealer in Lakeland, where part of his responsibilities was to order the toys. "One of the best parts of that job was the access to information and toys that the average collector doesn't have," he says. Some of that information came from attending John Deere dealer meetings. "Ertl would always set up a big booth with their current toys, and they always had a couple of prototype tractors that hadn't been introduced yet. These prototypes were in 1/8 scale. I never knew they made prototypes that size and then scaled them down to 1/16. They were really huge, and identical to the Precision tractors. I was impressed with how detailed they were.

"They kept them in glass cases and display cases so you couldn't handle them and touch them, but it was still exciting and interesting. They weren't looking for any feedback, but just wanted to show them off, and let dealers know what was coming up, and give the dealers a better idea of what went into the designing and production of toys. I remember the 4020 narrow-front-end prototype in particular. They had it there not to get more orders, but just as a conversation piece. They built just a few of the prototypes, so it's hard to know what they're worth, if you had one of them."

The Overall Picture

The question remains: How is it decided that one tractor comes out in 1/16, and another in 1/64?

"What we're looking to do," says Ertl's Becker, "is present a balanced line of products in each scale. So while we can't do every product in every scale, we're going to look at what parts of our line need new product, and try to allocate it as best as we can, relative to where the manufacturer—like John Deere—would like to see it, and where we would like to see it. John Deere might come to us and say, 'We would like to do this in 1/64 scale.'

"So it's what our current line looks like, and what we see happening in the coming years, where we see opportunities, or where if we're overloaded in one scale we might try to go to another scale for a product that's next up."

Collectors also have an effect on the market, Becker says. "We keep in mind the amount we're asking collectors to purchase each year. We try to make our decisions by keeping in mind, 'Are we asking collectors to overextend themselves? Are we being reasonable to what we're asking them to purchase?' By doing that, sometimes we will go into different scales, so not everything is a higher-priced 1/16 item."

And certain tractors lend themselves to certain lines. "When we talk about our Precision Line of tractors," explained Becker, "we are purposely looking for tractors that will be able to show a large amount of detail. If it doesn't come off as precision detailed, a tractor totally covered up by the body, there's less to show off in terms of the different parts. For Precision tractors, we're looking for items that will do best with all the detail shown."

Collector Updike says Carter & Gruenewald sell toys for Scale Models and Ertl both, and he likes to pay attention to the toys they sell. "It's interesting to

Ertl catalog
In 1964, Ertl offered a variety of 1/16 tractors, including these International Harvester and Oliver replicas made of a combination of die-cast aluminum and die-cast zinc.

see how a toy gets transposed from 1/16 scale down to 1/64, how details are lost or added. I think it's neat to see how size determines what's done in a tractor. One thing they don't do is just reduce a 1/16 scale model toy to 1/64. There are a lot of details that can't be put in just because of the smaller size."

Collectors tend to look for "branded" tractors, like John Deere or Case, according to Becker. "They have specific interests. For kids," he says, "there's less concern for the name brand, so I could do a tractor and color it green, or a tractor and color it red, and for a child playing in a sandbox and using it as a toy, he would be apt to be happy with it. That's not to say that no kid wants a John Deere tractor just like dad. But you're going to see that the adult is almost always concerned with the brand of tractor, because they're buying it for a collection."

Farm equipment manufacturers help determine the sizes of some tractors in another way. Becker says,

"Sometimes John Deere might want to use a tractor as a giveaway. They want it to have some perception of the value, and certainly the size relates to the perceived value of the product." So 1/16 might be used for a giveaway as it would seem solid and valuable, where a 1/64 might come across just the opposite.

"In other cases, there's just kind of a belief that we've traditionally done certain kinds of things in certain scales, and there's a traditional scale for a certain type of tractor, or implement, or construction item," Becker finishes. "Collector tractors are done in a variety of scales."

Future Size Changes

So, will other scales develop in the future? "There's always that possibility," says Ertl's Willey. "But I don't see the Ertl Company creating any new scales. If we addressed it, it would be something that already had a reason for being. We aren't going to go out and make like something in 1/57 scale just to create a new scale. That definitely is not something we would want to do."

He said Ertl had a collector conference, "a marketing focus group, if you will, with collectors at a recent National Farm Toy Show, and one of the things that was important to collectors was that the manufacturers don't create new sizes just to create a new market. So obviously, we don't think that would be a very intelligent route to take."

In the end, the process is much more planned than many people might think. "We spend all year trying to plan it," Becker says. "While collectors go to shows once in a while, we're doing it day in and day out, and trying to figure out what makes sense."

When farm toy people possess the tractors and implements they want, and perhaps a few farm animals, the next logical step is to set those toys in a scene.

Some scenes are ready made in the form of farm sets, like Ertl's Massey-Ferguson die-cast set made in 1/16 in 1965. It contains a Massey-Ferguson 175 tractor with disc, plow, spreader, and wagon. Or a Monarch Plastics Case set, with a Model SC Case tractor and a two-wheel spreader in 1/16. Or a Scale Models Oliver set, with an Oliver 1855 tractor with disc, plow, and trailer.

But the weakness in the farm sets is that they are generic and don't possess a true sense of individual authenticity. That's where homemade farm scenes come in. In these farm scenes, the farmstead is viewed from above: miniature houses, barns, silos, pens, vehicles, fields—everything that makes up the typical farm. Other people make the farm scene to correspond with the farm on which they grew up, or a farm to which they hold a particularly strong attachment. In their own way, the farm scenes are just like playing in the sand again, but acceptable for adults.

Ron Fuerstenberg of Worthington, Minnesota, wrote in the November 1996 issue of *Toy Farmer* that "I have a replica of the farm I grew up on mounted on a 4-foot-by-8-foot [120x240-cm] sheet of plywood and includes an alfalfa field being cut, raked and baled; a bean field being disked, plated, cultivated and combined; and a cornfield being picked by a pull-type two-row picker and a picker mounted on a Farmall."

"I got into collecting toy tractors by building the replica of the farm my dad and my uncle owned and farmed together. I started by making the buildings out of cardboard. Later, I made them out of wood. After I had the buildings made, I decided I needed some tractors to go along with them. I started looking for toys similar to the equipment we had on the farm."

There is a wide variety of farm toy scenes that can be made, showing vehicles planting, harvesting, putting up hay, or any of the myriad other jobs being done on the farm. Sometimes these scenes are static, mimicking action, such as having the chain tight between one tractor pulling out another, or the box of a dump truck lifted and half-full of rice used as grain.

Sometimes parts of the scenes actually move, as in Michael Brasda's farm scene. This Poynette, Wisconsin, collector created a scene in which the wheels of the tractor spin as it tries to pull another out of the muck, or an auger moves grain from a truck into a bin, all run by batteries or regular electricity. The only limit is a person's imagination.

Often some of the buildings have been made by hand to resemble remembered buildings, while normally the vehicles placed within these scenes are farm toys that were bought as opposed to those which a person might make. Brasda said he got interested in farm scenes after his father built him a barn years ago, with individual bricks and open stanchions inside the barn. Now, the 220-pound (99-kg) display contains thirty-eight different moving parts.

While he was pondering how to make his scene come alive, he was told he should use toy stock-car track. "I said I didn't want a car show, though. I wanted to make it work, make it move, without anyone seeing or knowing how it works. I take pride in what I do. If you have a motor sticking out, then it's not realistic and not acceptable."

In addition to his buildings and vehicles, he has a fish pond with live minnows in his farm scene. "I've seen water running on other scenes in other displays, but I've never seen running water that looked realistic. I saw someone take a half-inch hose, with water shooting out of it in a current stronger than I've seen in any river realistically. I want all of mine to be realistic."

As a realistic farm, Brasda's includes a farmhouse, barn, and quonset with the roof off, garage, farm animals—including pigs, sheep, horses, beef and dairy cows, fish, chickens, and geese—even people, but not a cat. "They don't make cats, I guess," he says.

And, of course, Brasda's scene includes farm machinery. Among his machinery is a combine with a head that goes around. "To do it so no one would see how it moved, I got a little bitty thin brass gear, probably 1/60,000 inch wide, the same diameter as the outside diameter of the combine reel. It just blended in nice. It leads down below to a small gear to another to another to a jackshaft to a homemade pulley, using a piece of special belting I made up, to the main drive that runs everything else."

He also has a lit semi-truck. "There are fifty running lights made with fiber-optics on the trailer. The tractor has eighty-four lights."

What people like most is that everything moves, he says, and it was most graphically displayed at one toy show a couple of years ago. "I was talking to one of the vendors about it, and told him to come over and look at it, but he could never get closer than three-deep people from it. Then a fuse blew out. I had only one fuse running the thing then, and I didn't have an extra. The vendor miraculously got the front row, because everybody else just walked away. And I only had about fifteen things moving at the time.

"My intent was to make it realistic. People usually say, 'This is my fifth time back and I still find something new every time.' They don't look, or something doesn't catch their eye, and I've made things so they move only once in a while. There are thirty-eight moving things on the board at present. I've thought of half a dozen things I'm going to change. I never do anything simple," he laughs. "I've always got to do it complicated."

Rick Campbell of Apple River, Illinois, made a different type of farm scene with moving parts. As a kid, he ventured much further into the pretend world of farm toys than most kids, building a town with roads, houses, implement dealers, and even a working water system. "We never had a sandbox," Campbell says. "But in our back yard in Watertown, Minnesota, my dad, who owned a construction business with my uncle, had a couple of stockpiles of gravel for people who needed it in a hurry. One of them was under a shade tree, and we just kind of took it over, my brother and I and two of the neighbor boys."

They built a regular town in the sand pile. At the top, they had a water reservoir lined with asbestos shingles so the water wouldn't soak into the gravel right away. At the lower side of the gravel pile was another reservoir.

This was before the days of seamless pop and beer cans, so they took the ones that had seams in the top and bottom, cut them out with can openers, and made

pipes out of the cans. "We buried the cans just like real, end to end, and at three intersections we had one coming up, with a cover on it, a manhole that we could look down into. We would fill the upper reservoir with a five-gallon pail of water, open the gates, and watch it run through. We had it tapped off to all the little businesses and everything. We got quite involved in our playing, quite realistic."

They had designated fields and businesses, and each player had his own business. "I had the implement dealership there in the gravel pile," Campbell laughs. "I had tractors and machinery, and sold that stuff in a pretend way."

They also took concrete field tile, stacked up a couple of them, and put grass clippings and wheat seeds in, and covered them up. "It would actually ferment. We never tried to drink any of the stuff," Campbell laughs. "We'd throw it down the ravine or into the compost pile. Oh, it was so much fun playing with toys back then."

Ertl Waterloo Boy
A die-cast Ertl 1/16 Waterloo Boy in front of a farm diorama. Collection: State Historical Society of Wisconsin.

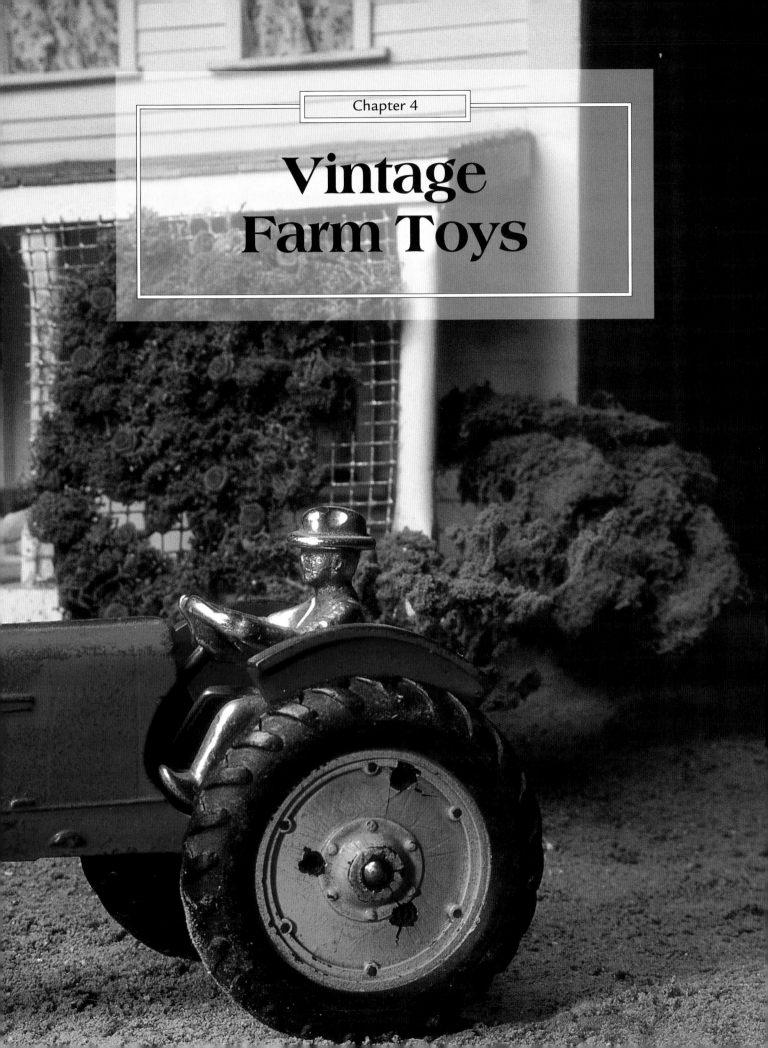

Chapter 4

Vintage Farm Toys

Toy historian Lillian Gottschalk, writing in *American Toy Cars & Trucks*, summed up the allure of vintage farm toys: "Boys who played with cars and trucks in the 1920s had toy tractors, too. They could be used in the fields to play farmer, to harvest crops, to load trucks, to tow things. Plows, rakes and trailers could be attached. When seen at antique meets today, they evoke remembrances and stories."

The vintage farm toys dating from the 1880s through World War II were predominantly made of cast iron, although there were notable exceptions, including the tin toys made by Louis Marx and the rubber toys of Auburn. These toys were made first and foremost as toys, compared with many of the post–World War II farm toys that were made for a growing market of collectors.

In the Beginning Was Wilkins

Like many major names and companies involved in the manufacture of farm toys, James S. Wilkins entered the toy business by accident. In 1880, Wilkins established the Triumph Wringer Company in Keene, New Hampshire, to manufacture washing machine wringers. As a lark, he also designed and produced toy washing machines and cast-iron locomotives. This sideline burgeoned so quickly that in just a couple of years he abandoned the real wringer business to craft toys.

In about 1886, Wilkins produced his first farm toys: a 1/16 cast-iron horse-drawn mower, sulky plow, hay rake, and tedder. These four Wilkins toys broke new ground, and they are generally acknowledged as the first farm toys commercially produced in the United States.

An 1889 article in a Keene newspaper heralded Wilkins's new venture: "A short time since a display of goods . . . called local attention to a novel and interesting branch of business which has with little observation by any one here grown into extensive proportions. We refer to the manufacture of the 'Wilkins Model Iron Toys.'. . . Mr. Wilkins has gotten out a number of patents on these toys and has quite a number in hand for the coming year." The newspaper reported that, at the time, Wilkins was selling as much as twenty-seven tons (24,300 kg) of toys per week.

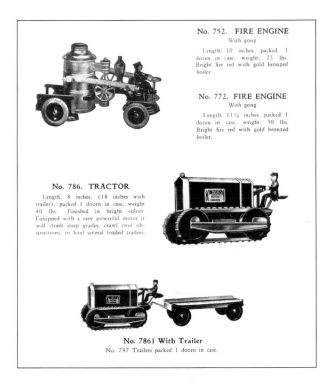

Kingsbury crawler catalog page
The Kingsbury Manufacturing Company of Keene, New Hampshire, superseded Wilkins and offered its "motor driven" No. 786 tractor in the 1920s. The crawler measured 8 inches (200 mm) long, and was available with an optional trailer.

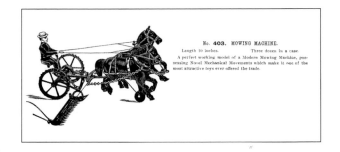

Wilkins mower catalog page
Wilkins's mower measured 10 inches (250 mm) long and possessed "Novel Mechanical Movements which make it one of the most attractive toys ever offered."

Arcade Oliver 70
Previous page: *In 1940, Arcade manufactured this red, cast-iron Oliver 70 tractor, which measures 5½ inches (138 mm) long, and has a narrow front end and nickel-plated driver.*

Wilkins horse rake

Above: *The Wilkins Toy Company of Keene, New Hampshire, offered this cast-iron No. 404 horse rake in the 1880s and 1890s. It measured 9 inches (225 mm) long. Collection: Ray Lacktorin. (Photograph by Michael Dregni)*

Wilkins sulky plow

Left: *Wilkins's No. 410 sulky plow measured 10½ inches (263 mm) long. As the catalog promised, it was "a clever toy which gives all the practical ideas of the working of a full size plow." Collection: Ray Lacktorin. (Photograph by Michael Dregni)*

The newspaper reporter also offered a rare insight into Wilkins's methods and the care he put into his toys. "Iron toys have been made for a number of years, but in a very crude manner, and lacking in correct shape and proportions, until Mr. Wilkins embarked in their manufacture. He takes the ground that a toy is an educator, and in designing them he adheres strictly to reproducing in miniature the article which the toy represents, never slighting any detail that will correctly impress the eye."

In 1895, the Wilkins firm was purchased by Harry Thayer Kingsbury's Kingsbury Manufacturing Company, which retained Wilkins's factory in Keene. Kingsbury continued to make toys under the Wilkins banner until 1919, when the name was changed to Kingsbury. Under the new moniker, the firm manufactured several farm toys, including the "Little Jim" tractor, and other farm toys. Kingsbury ceased toy production in 1942.

Today, James Wilkins's pioneering cast-iron farm toys are an important piece of toy tractor history. They are all rare and can sell in the late 1990s for as much as $3,500 for the mower, $4,200 for the sulky plow, $5,000 for the hay rake, and $6,500 for the tedder.

Arcade Toys: "They Look Real"

The Arcade Manufacturing Company, like many early toy companies in general and farm toy companies in particular, was founded not to make toys, but to produce other farm-related products. In the case of Arcade, the firm made feed grinders, plows, and other agricultural materials for the agricultural area around its home base in Freeport, Illinois.

Arcade's roots date back to the 1868 founding of the Novelty Iron Works, one of the first industries in Freeport, by brothers E. H. and Charles Morgan with financing from J. B. Hazen. The fledgling firm produced a variety of farm products including water pumps and windmills, soon followed by box coffee mills and iron sections used for store fronts and flooring. The company moved to the Arcade Addition of Freeport in 1885, from which it borrowed its new name, the Arcade Manufacturing Company.

Arcade's manufacturing of toys began as a sideline. Rather than waste the scrap lumber the company generated, E. H. Morgan thought there should be a use for it; he decided to make toy versions of the firm's coffee mills. He never would he guessed that the cof-

Arcade advertisement
Arcade cast-iron farm toys were made in Freeport, Illinois, and are highly prized by the modern-day collector. The Fordson tractor shown on the left was made in several colors and sizes by Arcade in 1924, the date of this Farm Mechanics *magazine ad.*

fee mill would be the first of 300 different and highly esteemed toys the company would produce, mostly in cast iron, over the next seventy-eight years.

By the early 1900s, Arcade needed a fifty-page catalog to show all its toys. It is thought that Arcade's first farm toy was not manufactured until 1920: an Oliver two-bottom pull-type cast-iron plow. However, another reference said the plow was not manufactured until 1926. If the latter date is correct, then Arcade's first farm toy was made in 1925: a cast-iron McCormick-Deering 10/20 tractor in three versions, with spoke wheels, slip-on tires, or white-rubber tires.

In 1924, Arcade released a Yellow Cab toy, and although it was not a farm toy, it was arguably Arcade's most famous toy. Its production began a huge and successful line of automotive toys for the company.

In 1926, Arcade dramatically expanded its manufacture of farm toys by releasing four new cast-iron tractors. The first was an unidentified row-crop tractor that was 3¼ inches long (81.25 mm). This was followed by a pair of Fordsons, one measuring 4¾ inches (118.75 mm) in length, the other 6 inches (150 mm). The larger Fordson came with or without lugs on its rear wheels.

Arcade farm truck
One of the most prized farm trucks is this Arcade stake truck, of which several kinds were made in the 1920s. Notice the Arcade sticker remaining on the door of this example. (Photograph by Bill Vossler)

Arcade Fordson F
This green Fordson F was made by Arcade in 1928 and is a variant color of those made by the company in cast iron. The tractor measures 4¾ inches (119 mm) long, but many of Arcade's toys were not made to a particular scale. Other similar variants of the Arcade Fordson F include a variety of colors; lengths, including 3⅞, 5¾, and 6 inches (97, 144, and 150 mm); as well as variations of rear wheels with or without lugs. Collection: Brad Johnson. (Photograph by Bill Vossler)

Farm Mechanics Arcade advertisement

Above: Farm Mechanics *magazine offered free Arcade toys in the late 1920s and early 1930s as an incentive to lure new subscribers. This ad from November 1930 detailed six Arcade-made International Harvester toys that were available alongside Vindex John Deere and Case toys.*

Arcade McCormick-Deering 10/20

Above: *This 1/16 McCormick-Deering 10/20 tractor was manufactured by Arcade in 1925. It was available in three variations: spoked wheels, white rubber tires, or cast-iron wheels with slip-on tires, as with this version. This toy tractor has also been repainted, which drops its value considerably from the $500 it could have brought if original. A new screw also holds the rear wheel to the back hub, another sign that this toy has been restored. Collection: State Historical Society of Wisconsin.*

Arcade Allis-Chalmers WC

Left: *In 1940, Arcade debuted this bright-orange Allis-Chalmers WC cast-iron tractor with a removable nickel-plated driver. The tractor measured 7⅜ inches (184 mm) long and has a narrow front end. New in box (NIB), it sold for roughly $1,650 in the 1990s. (Photograph by Bill Vossler)*

Arcade also manufactured three plows in 1926: a McCormick-Deering plow with a red frame, yellow wheels, and a bronzed-aluminum plow; and two Oliver plows. One was red with nickel-plated wheels and bronzed-aluminum plowshares, and was 6¾ inches (168.75 mm) long. The other was red enamel with nickel-plated wheels and blades of striped aluminum bronze; it was a quarter inch shorter at 6½ inches (162 mm) long.

During the late 1920s, the popular *Farm Mechanics* magazine began offering a free toy for every three-year subscription, which cost one dollar. Arcade supplied the magazine with its McCormick-Deering Weber Wagon as a giveaway, although the Arcade wagon required two subscriptions.

During its heyday from the 1920s through the 1940s, Arcade made more than two dozen toy tractors, including Allis-Chalmers, Oliver, Farmall, and John Deere models; a variety of farm implements, including an Oliver plant and spreader; a McCormick-Deering threshing machine; and a Fairbanks-Morse Model Z portable engine. Also among Arcade's list of farm toys was a red Allis-Chalmers tractor with a green trailer; a Farmall A tractor; and a gray-and-red Arcade threshing machine that was 10 inches long (250 mm).

It was in the 1920s that Arcade adopted the slogan, "They Look Real," "in keeping," wrote Gottschalk in *American Toy Cars & Trucks*, "with its program and policy to adopt the shape and color of articles and vehicles from real life as models for its toys."

Also during this period, Arcade's toy production became completely mechanized. Gottschalk wrote, "Toys moved from molding machines to a tumbler where rough edges and sprues [waste metal left where molten metal had been poured through holes into the mold] were removed. Poorly fitting parts were repaired and parts were plated where required. Moving to an assembly room, the toys were fastened with rivets and then painted either by dipping or spraying. A decal was applied after drying and during the final inspection. Most Arcade toys have the name cast into the toy."

Owing to metal restrictions during World War II, Arcade ceased making toys for good in 1942. In 1946, the company was sold to the Rockwell Manufacturing Company of Buffalo, New York.

Arcade McCormick-Deering 10/20
Arcade made this McCormick-Deering 10/20. Arcade's toys were typically listed by their actual physical size—6 inches (150 mm) in length, in this case—rather than being designated as a scale of 1/16 or 1/20. (Photograph by Bill Vossler)

Arcade International Harvester creamer

Left: *In 1930, Arcade made this 1/12 International Harvester cream separator, which can sell for $1,300 in top-notch condition in the 1990s. This one is complete with the original cream pail. Collection: Jim Goke. (Photograph by Bill Vossler)*

Arcade Farmall M

Below: *Detail of a 1940 Arcade 1/16 Farmall M cast-iron tractor with painted engine components.*

Arcade John Deere A
*Arcade produced this 1/16 John Deere
A cast-iron tractor in 1940. The driver
is nickel-plated.*

72

Hubley Avery 18/36
This cast-iron Avery 18/36 tractor was made by the Hubley Manufacturing Company of Lancaster, Pennsylvania, in 1920. It measures only 4½ inches (113 mm) long. Collection: National Toy Farm Museum.

Hubley Toys: "They're Different"

"They're Different" was the motto for the high-quality toys from the Hubley Manufacturing Company of Lancaster, Pennsylvania. Founded by John E. Hubley, the firm was first listed in the city directory in 1894, when a factory owned by Hubley and other investors manufactured electric toy train equipment and components.

Through the years, Hubley made a wide variety of toys, turning to cast iron in 1909, after a disastrous fire, financial problems, and the sale of the company to two former executives, John H. Hartmann and Joseph T. Breneman. Toys at that time included horse-drawn wagons and fire engines, miniature coal stoves, circus trains, and guns. Hubley soon added automotive toys to its line, and as the real automotive industry boomed, Hubley kept pace by adding more miniature automobiles until cars almost dominated the firm's line in the 1930s.

Hubley's first foray into farm toys was with a 4½-inch-long (112-mm), round-radiator Avery tractor in 1920. Hubley's 8-inch-long (200-mm) farm trailer with gate is the firm's most common farm toy. The rarest Hubley farm toys are the 8½-inch-long (212-mm) cast-iron tractor shovel made in 1933, which can bring several thousand dollars, and the 8½-inch-long (212-mm) Fordson tractor with loader made in 1938, which can bring almost as much.

Though Hubley isn't thought of as a farm toy company, it did make other farm toys: a 5½-inch-long (137-mm) cast-iron Fordson F tractor with crank and driver from the late 1930s; a tractor simply called a "Junior" of undetermined vintage; a cast-iron Oliver 70 Orchard tractor with fenders over the rear wheels released in 1938; a 5¼-inch-long (131.25-mm) unidentified yellow tractor; a plastic tractor and farmer; a 7-inch-long (175-mm) cast-iron stockyard truck #851 from the 1940s; two die-cast Ford 961 Powermaster tractors in 1961, one a row-crop, one not; a Ford 961 Select-O-Speed made in 1961; 1/12 Ford 4000 and 6000 tractors produced in 1963; a die-cast Ford Commander 6000 in 1963.

Hubley still makes toys in the 1990s, although its line does not include farm toys.

Hubley Farmall M

Above: *This steerable Farmall M was made by Hubley in die-cast steel in 1952. This 1/12 model has a narrow front end, and the name "Hubley" in raised letters on its side. Collection: State Historical Society of Wisconsin.*

Hubley Ford 900

Right: *Hubley made this 1/12 Ford 900 series Kiddie Toy die-cast tractor in the 1950s. Tractors like these are not always extremely popular with collectors because they represent a tractor series, rather than an exact model, like a Ford 961, for instance. Collection: State Historical Society of Wisconsin.*

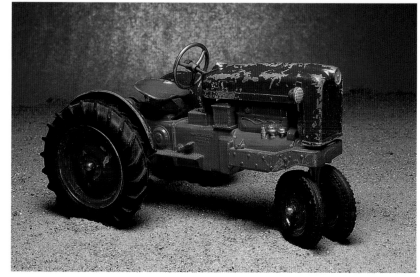

Vindex Toys

Vindex was an interesting farm toy company. First, it was not actually a toy "company," according to Harold D. Neff, a former executive with the National Sewing Machine Company of Belvidere, Illinois. Neff set the record straight in a letter to the Boone County Historical Society in Belvidere: "Actually there never was a Vindex Toy Company, but a line of cast-iron toys and novelties, including some banks, which were manufactured by National Sewing Machine Company."

Farm toys were not even part of National's program prior to 1930, when it was manufacturing 500 Family Sewing Machines and 250 washing machines daily. When the Great Depression struck, sales of National's main products plummeted, and in a fight to survive, the company turned to manufacturing other products. "So we began to produce other lines of goods that would give work to our people, and retain as many as we could," said Neff. National adopted a complete line of Home Work Shop Machinery—lathes, band saws, jig saws, saw tables, and line shaft assemblies—to keep its people working. Neff wrote, "We also decided to produce a line of Cast Iron Toys and Novelties, so we employed a model maker, and started."

Neff was put in charge of the manufacture and sale of the new toy line. When the time came to name the toys, company officials thought Vindex was an unusual name and chose it. Vindex had been the original name of some of their sewing machines. Vindex toys and novelties included bookends, table lamps, dog doorstops, dog and owl banks, horse-drawn wagons, and farm machinery. Several hundred thousand dog doorstops were made by the fifty people employed to produce the Vindex line.

One of those workers in the 1930s was Wade Leaich of Belvidere. "Everybody else who worked there was much older than I was. I had to leave high school at the end of my sophomore year," he says, "because my parents couldn't afford books or clothes for school. My dad was unemployed." The fifteen-year-old Leaich approached National, claiming he was seventeen so they would consider him for a job. He was hired on December 11, 1936, as a setup man for machining Vindex toys.

Each Vindex toy had exact requirements explains Leaich: "The blueprint called for certain dimensions on the parts, and if they wanted a hole drilled in the part and a tap, they told you what size tap went in there and the depth of the thread. So it was my job to set up the machine to run that part."

The screw machine, lathe, or milling machine all had to be set to different specifications for different

Vindex Bates Steel Mule
Vindex's 1/16 Bates Steel Mule measured 6½ inches (163 mm) long.

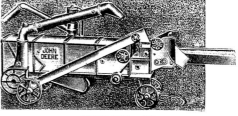

Vindex John Deere thresher
Vindex's John Deere thresher was a full 15 inches (375 mm) long.

Vindex John Deere D

Above: *The National Sewing Machine Company produced this Vindex John Deere D tractor from cast iron in 1930. The driver and pulley were nickel plated. This standard model has a wide front end, and is worth about $2,400 in excellent condition in the 1990s.*

toys. When a new toy came out—like the Case Manure Spreader farm toy #74—the machines had to be recalibrated, which was also one of Wade's jobs.

"These toys were made in parts, which had to be riveted together. All these parts had to pivot, like the front axle on the John Deere tractor, and the casting that the axle went through pivoted also, so the front wheels would turn, like the steering wheel in your car. There were quite a few different operations to learn to make toys, including farm toys, and it was kind of difficult, but I needed a job, so I figured I'd better get busy and learn it, so I did." He worked there six years and left when he got a raise elsewhere that National could not meet.

Among Vindex's farm toys was a John Deere three-bottom plow, Deere manure spreader, Deere wagon, and a team of horses. Vindex also made a series of trucks and race cars, as well as motorcycles, a Belvidere blimp, mail plane, and Fokker Planes #40 and #90, which are rare toys.

The Fokker Planes bring up another story, offering insight into Vindex manufacturing methods. One day, Wade was told to separate rejected cast iron and steel parts in barrels so the cast iron could be remelted for sewing machine heads. Among poorly made or broken cast-iron parts of farm toys in the barrel, he found parts for a Fokker airplane. "I put the parts together myself, took it to the paint shop, and they didn't know what color to paint it because those planes had never gone into production."

Afterward, he took it to the contract order department to buy it. "The guy said, 'We don't even have it listed, so just give me a quarter and I'll write out a slip for you to take it out.'" That quarter was a full hour's pay for Wade.

Fifty years later, Wade sold the Fokker at auction for $1,750, and in one fell swoop realized more money from the airplane than he had made in three years of work at National at twenty-five cents an hour.

For Wade, making Vindex toys was more than a job. During those times, women worked eight-hour days and men ten-hour days. "After the women would go home, I'd usually go out to one of the machines for the last two hours of my shift, and put the Vindex toys

Vindex John Deere horsedrawn manure spreader

Below: *This Vindex toy of 1930 vintage is a 1/16 John Deere horse-drawn manure spreader made of cast iron. This manure spreader can fetch about $3,500 in the 1990s. (Photograph by Bill Vossler)*

together," he says, "because it was fun."

In 1938, National stopped making Vindex toys altogether, because, Wade said, the union was demanding wages that were too high—"a minimum of forty cents an hour."

Considering the premium placed on original boxes for farm toys nowadays, collectors searching for original Vindex boxes are out of luck. Vindex toys were wrapped in oil paper, taped, wrapped in corrugated cardboard, and taped again. Boxes were not used.

Another interesting sidelight to the Vindex story is how the toys were sold. During the Great Depression, many farm families could not afford to buy farm toys, new or used. For industrious children, salvation came by way of *Farm Mechanics* magazine, which offered Vindex cast-iron toys for selling subscriptions.

The scarcity of some Vindex toys today may be explained by the *Farm Mechanics* subscription prizes.

The rare John Deere combine (#86) was described tantalizingly in a Vindex catalog of the day as "cutter and reel operate; imitation motor exhaust; painted in John Deere colors; removable man." For a kid to obtain the Deere combine, they were required to sell five three-year subscriptions to the magazine at a cost of one dollar per three-year subscription. With money so scarce during the Depression, it was much easier for youngsters to earn the toy Case tractor (#36, "equipped with power pulley; removable nickeled driver; lug rear wheels"), which required but a single three-year subscription. Partly for this reason, many more Vindex Case tractors exist today than John Deere combines.

Farm Mechanics also offered a Vindex toy hay rack (#89, "front and rear standards collapse; green and red") for two subscriptions; and the Vindex John Deere hay loader (#85, "revolving chains and teeth; positive drive

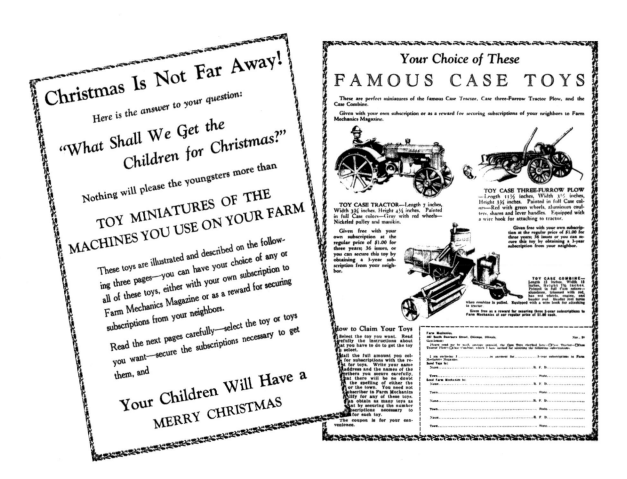

Farm Mechanics Vindex advertisement
Farm Mechanics *magazine offered free farm toys in the late 1920s and early 1930s as an incentive for subscriptions. This ad from November 1930 detailed three Vindex Case toys that were available alongside Vindex John Deere and Arcade International Harvester toys.*

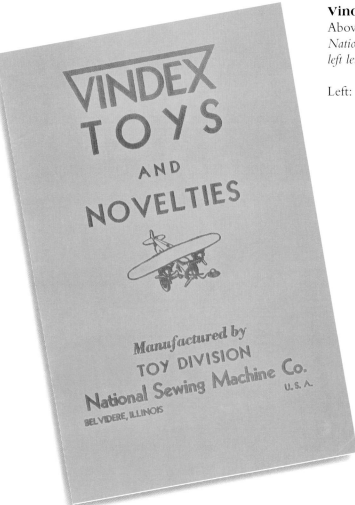

Vindex Case plow
Above: *This Vindex Case three-bottom plow was made by the National Sewing Machine Company in 1930. Note that the left lever has broken off this toy. (Photograph by Bill Vossler)*

Left: **1920s Vindex catalog**

wheels") and John Deere thresher (#88, "removable straw stacker and grain pipe; loose drive pulley") for three subscriptions each. Occasionally the seller's own subscription to *Farm Mechanics* counted to help "purchase" toys, as with the toy John Deere gas engine (#79, "pulley and fly wheels operate; a real replica of Deere Farm Engine"). For others, like the rare ones, only other people's subscriptions counted.

Today, Vindex toys are valuable collectibles. "They're expensive and hard to find," notes collector Bob Beall of Twelve Point, Indiana. "Some of them cost as much as a new car." He isn't sure he'll ever be able to afford them. "So I just enjoy them when I see that someone else has them."

Dale Johansen of Latimer, Iowa, is on the other side of the fence. He owned 140 cast-iron toys, including toys from Vindex, Arcade, Stanley, "a little bit of everything. I had a cast-iron manure spreader when I was a kid, and I've got one just like it right now. I had a John Deere Vindex three-bottom plow, and I've got one of those now too. I've got forty-seven cast-iron tractors, and the rest are implements, threshing machines, trucks, everything."

Johansen has been lucky in finding cast-iron toys that were cast off as times changed. "At the public dump years ago," he says. "you wouldn't believe what people used to throw away. I'd find them there and then take them home and fix them up."

Vindex John Deere D and Van Brunt grain drill

Right: *This 1/16 John Deere D tractor and Van Brunt grain drill were made by the National Sewing Machine Company. The belt pulley and driver were nickel-plated on the Deere. The scarce grain drill model had separate discs. (Photograph by Bill Vossler)*

Vindex John Deere–Van Brunt grain drill

Facing page, bottom: *Vindex offered this finely detailed 1/16 Van Brunt grain drill that measured 9¾ inches (244 mm) long. Collection: Ray Lacktorin. (Photograph by Michael Dregni)*

Vindex John Deere combine

Above: *This 1/16 cast-iron Vindex John Deere combine with a standing operator was made in 1930. Today, it is a true treasure: In the 1990s, it can sell for nearly $6,000. Collection: Ray Lacktorin. (Photograph by Michael Dregni)*

Vindex Case combine catalog page

Right: *Vindex also offered a 1/16 Case combine that measured 12¼ inches (306 mm) long.*

CASE COMBINE

COLORS

CASE GALVANIZE AND RED

Imitation motor exhaust.
Cutter reel revolves.

Packed one in a carton

Shipping weight, 7½ pounds

TOY NO. 73

Length, 12¼"; width, 8"; height, 7½".

Price $36.00 a dozen

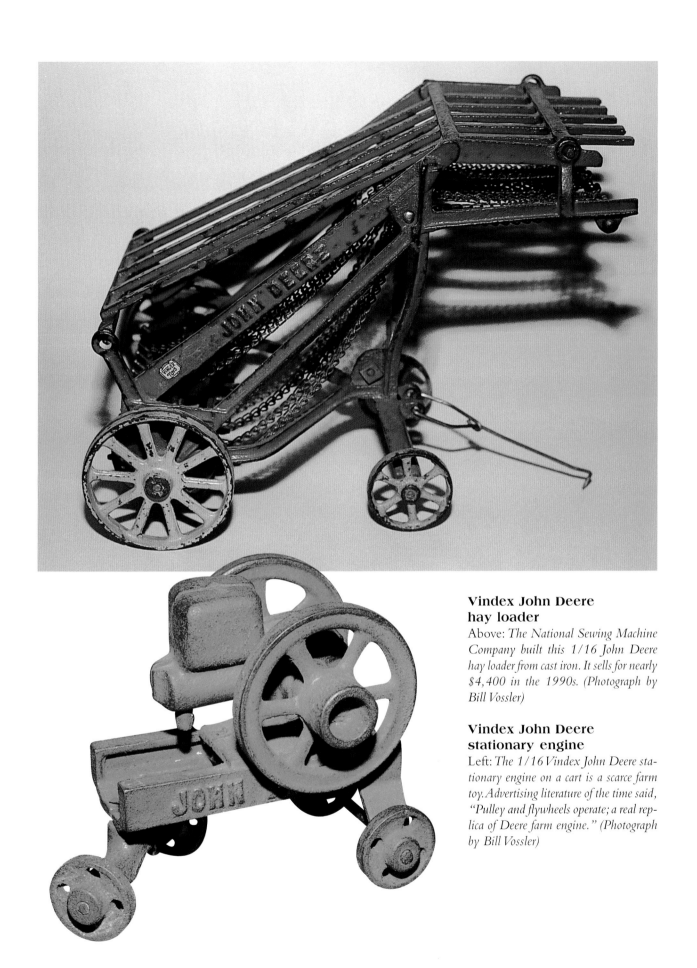

**Vindex John Deere
hay loader**

Above: *The National Sewing Machine
Company built this 1/16 John Deere
hay loader from cast iron. It sells for nearly
$4,400 in the 1990s. (Photograph by
Bill Vossler)*

**Vindex John Deere
stationary engine**

Left: *The 1/16 Vindex John Deere stationary engine on a cart is a scarce farm
toy. Advertising literature of the time said,
"Pulley and flywheels operate; a real replica of Deere farm engine." (Photograph
by Bill Vossler)*

If real tractors pull real implements in real life, then farm toy collectors are going to desire replica implements too. An "implement" is pretty much anything that is not a tractor or truck.

When collector Jerrold Sundstrom of Oriska, North Dakota, was a kid, he didn't care for tractors. "My great love has always been combines. I always wanted to be with someone who was driving a combine. To me as a kid, it was fascinating. In one end goes all the plants, and out the other end comes a bunch of dust and the grain is in the hopper. How was that possible?"

Sundstrom liked to stay out with his dad on the combine. "I was only seven or eight, and there were no cabs, but I liked to sit there on the combine. People thought I was crazy." About age eleven, he started driving combines.

Like most collectors, Sundstrom started collecting a little bit of everything. But after his father died, he held a farm toy auction. "I decided I was going to specialize. I had thought there were only a few combines, and I'd collect all of them, but when you get out there you find out there are a lot more combines than you think."

He narrowed his choices to Oliver, Minneapolis-Moline, and Cockshutt, "all of which were tied in to White Farm Equipment. I thought the combines wouldn't be too hard to keep up with, but I found out there were way more brands, varieties, and versions than I'd realized."

Collector Lyle Hovland says he's glad he got into the implement line early. "In the early days a lot of guys didn't collect implements. They were secondary at first. But implements are more collectible now, to support the total collection. Because there's more interest, I think that's a push for Ertl and others to make more of them."

Marvin Fredrick of Oconomowoc, Wisconsin, says he used to have a lot of farm implements, "but I've thinned down to just the ones I like. I've got most of the Oliver ones, a little bit of Massey-Harris, and I've got a lot of cast iron, although nothing Vindex. I've never had anything Vindex. I've got Fordson, pretty near the whole set of International

stuff there, except for the hay wagon, and a couple of Big Red trucks, as well as manure spreaders, one with steel wheels and one with rubber tires."

John Kayser of Dell Rapids, South Dakota, also collects implements. "I went to a sale once and didn't know diddly about what to pay, and I saw this real nice McCormick spreader. I paid thirty dollars, and I thought, man, I gotta be nuts. But today, I find out it was worth it. It's a really nice clean spreader. It was just luck that I found and bought some of those toys. You just can't find toys any more, hardly. Everybody has started collecting implements."

Toy historian Dick Sonnek prefers the implements made by Pro-Tractor Replicas of Mora, Minnesota. "They only make one or two of them a year. I like the uniqueness of them, because the qualities have never been offered in a similar toy by anyone else. I also like the quality of the workmanship, the detail on them, the accuracy."

Among Pro-Tractor Replicas's first implements were a horse-drawn culti-packer and horse-drawn single-row cultivator. Sonnek is also impressed by the firm's corn planter. "One thing I like about all of them is that they're all horse drawn, and really go a long ways back. I never harnessed a horse or drove any in my farming operation with the exception of once or twice, but I just like that older stuff."

Collector Don Lux of Janesville, Wisconsin, has a 1/16 Carter pull-type McCormick-Deering 7A disc harrow from 1950. "They were two and a half bucks each at the time, and I bought two of them. One my kids played with and wrecked over the years, but the other one I saved in the box. I saw where they're now selling for anywhere from $150 to $300 in mint condition. Actually, I've seen the boxes bringing more than the implements sometimes."

Lloyd Jark of Stratford, South Dakota, collects John Deere implements. "I like the combines, the digger line, manure spreaders, hay wagons, cotton pickers—anything that John Deere comes out with, I end up making a purchase of them. Maybe someday I'll find a big enough display room to show all of them," he laughs. "Then I'd hand them down to my grandchildren. For a lot of them who live out of state, these toys aren't available in their areas, because it's not a farming area like Iowa is."

Tru-Scale is one of the best companies for making farm toy implements, Ken Updike says. "Their choppers and balers had moving parts, and they made excellent plows."

Deter's Supercast of Spring Grove, Minnesota, produces precision-made models of modern implements, including a disc chisel plow, and a folding planter through White that really works. "It contains little cylinders, and is battery powered and runs on compressed air," according to Updike. "It's nice stuff, with everything nutted and screwed together like the real machines, not just molded in, but $700 for each of them is a nice chunk of change."

Gottman Toys of Missouri makes 1/16 Kinze grain carts, Kinze planters, and augers that work. They fold down and have the little inspection doors on the side covered by plexiglass. They also have detailed PTO drive lines. Updike says if it wasn't sitting on your table, you'd think it would really work. Scratchbuilder Ev Weber also does a nice job on his implements.

During the early stages of farm toy collecting, implements were not that important to most aficionados, but now they have come into their own, and they add that final dimension of reality and completeness to the farm toy scene.

BALES EJECT

(L. 14³/₄", W. 5³/₄", H. 3³/₈")

NO. 447 IH HAY BALER
PLAY FEATURES: Spring action ejects bales; wheel turns pickup teeth; rear drawbar pulls wagon; tongue hitches to tractors. Comes with 4 toy plastic bales **CONSTRUCTION:** Die-cast, rust-resistant Aluminum plus steel; plastic parts. Authentic scale replica IH red and white. Green bales.

Ertl International Harvester hay baler
Ertl made this 1/16 International Harvester hay baler with a spring action that ejected bales, as shown in this 1970 catalog. The baler was made from die-cast aluminum, and came with four green bales.

Topping New Idea manure spreader
This 1/16 1950 New Idea manure spreader was manufactured from plastic by Topping Models. Note the straight bar above the beaters; a second variation came with a slanted bar. Collection: State Historical Society of Wisconsin.

Reuhl Toys: "Designed for Rough Treatment"

Andy Reul started Reuhl Products in Madison, Wisconsin, in the late 1930s because he wanted to make accurate toy models of all kinds. He started by crafting boats and planes; in the late 1940s, he built his farm toys. Reul selected the corporate name "Reuhl" for ease of pronunciation.

The company motto was "Designed for Rough Treatment," later altered to "Designed for Rough Treatment and Wear." And Reuhl farm toys lived up to these words.

The first Reuhl farm toy was a Farmall Cub (T-3000), and as the company literature said, it was a plastic kit described as a "put-together" and "take-apart" toy, an exact miniature replica of International Harvester's Farmall Cub Tractor: "21 plastic parts. In display box. List $2.00; assembled in acetate case, list $4.00." Another advertisement for this toy said, "The Farmall Cub is like a game! Can you put together this toy?"

Reuhl's second farm toy was its Massey-Harris Clipper Combine from 1954, to which it purchased manufacturing rights. As Reul's friend Allan Hoover wrote in his history of Reuhl Products, *A Dream Comes True*, "Actually, this combine was first made by a foundry in Plymouth, Wisconsin. Reuhl bought the dies and made some design changes, resulting in the familiar Reuhl-Massey-Harris Clipper Combine."

The farm toy that Reuhl made in the greatest quantity was its Massey-Harris 44 tractor. The company received orders for 50,000 to 100,000 of the tractors annually from 1954 through 1958, according to Hoover.

Reuhl's Massey-Harris grain drill is one the firm's most sought-after toys. In fact, Hoover wrote in *A Dream Comes True*, "If your search for the ever-elusive Massey-Harris Grain Drill by Reuhl has been unsuccessful, it's for a very good reason: the toy was never put on the production line," Hoover wrote. "The misconception that such a piece exists probably stems from an artist's conception of the toy, which is included in this book. According to employees, Massey-Harris decided the tooling and production costs would be too high, so plans for the Grain Drill were dropped."

Some of the Reuhl toys have several variations. Reuhl's pull-type combine, for instance, was made in three different versions that were exactly alike except for the hitches: one featured a hitch that pointed up, one had a rotating hitch, and one hitch pointed down. Other toys had similar variations.

Reuhl went out of business in 1958 for a variety of reasons. The company had lucrative contracts with Caterpillar and Massey-Harris to make toys, but the licenses expired and were not renewed.

Reuhl's toys were also expensive for their time. Hoover wrote that with the exception of several powerful retailers such as Marshall Field & Company in

Reuhl Massey-Harris 44 parts list

The Massey-Harris 44 was the main-stay of Reuhl farm toys, and its most popular toy after its 1954 introduction. Although the tractor was expensive for its time at $3.50 in the 1950s, it garnered nearly a 100,000 orders annually for several years during the heyday of the company. Reuhl also made a 1/20 loader for the M-H 44 tractor. The loader, which came in two variations (with a wire trip rod or a ball chain trip rod), was made in 1954.

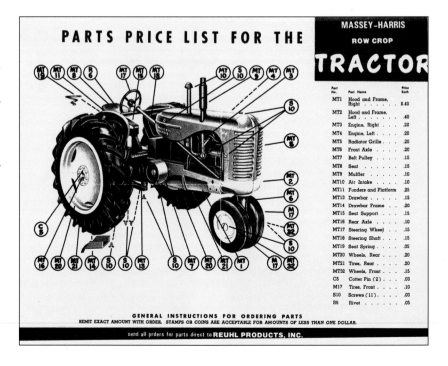

Reuhl Massey-Harris Clipper combine

Reuhl Products of Madison, Wisconsin, made this 1/20 Massey-Harris Clipper combine after buying the dies for the replica from a foundry in Plymouth, Wisconsin, which had originally produced the toy. Reuhl made changes before it brought out its much-sought-after version in 1954.

Farm toys also include trucks, which can be broken into two types: semi-trailer trucks and farm trucks.

Semi-rigs in 1/64 that pull different trailers with a agricultural company's name on the trailer are hot collectibles. "There's quite a bit of interest in those," collector Rick Campbell says. Among those of greatest interest are International Harvester trailers advertising Magnum tractors and Axial flow combines, or John Deere trailers advertising the 160th anniversary of John Deere and the 50th anniversary of self-propelled combines. "Really, anything that advertises for the farm implement manufacturer. The semis look like those that are used to haul farm parts," says Campbell.

Farm truck toys include cattle haulers, grain haulers, and flatbeds used to haul farm supplies. "The kind of trucks you'd see on a farm," Campbell says. Arcade was an early manufacturer of farm trucks with its Chevrolet and International stake trucks. Others included the Tonka Toys of Minnetonka, Minnesota, in the 1950s and 1960s, when the firm made grain and livestock haulers, among others. Ertl made farm trucks during the late 1960s through the early 1980s, while Structo also made farm trucks before they were bought out by Ertl.

Reuhl Massey-Harris 44

The Massey-Harris 44 was the mainstay of Reuhl farm toys and its most popular toy after its 1954 introduction. Alan Hoover, a family friend of company founder Andy Reul and author of a history of the firm, A Dream Comes True, *says the company received 50,000 to 100,000 orders for this tractor annually from 1954 through 1958. These are detailed tractors that came in a kit that required assembly.*

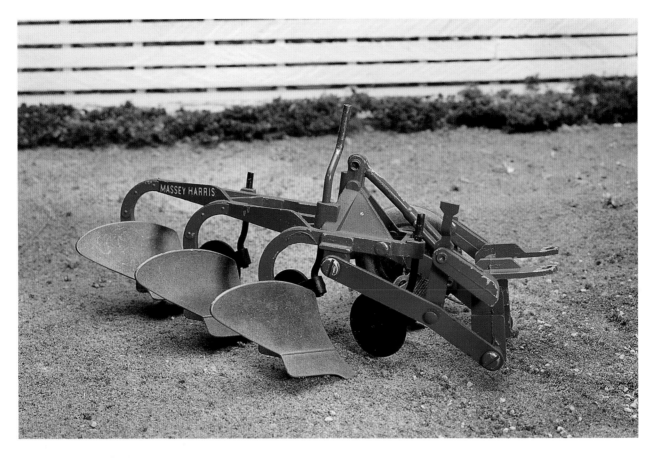

Reuhl Massey-Harris plow

Above: *Reuhl's die-cast 1/20 Massey-Harris three-bottom mounted plow was made in 1954 as a companion piece to fit the Massey-Harris 44 tractor. Some references list this and other Reuhl toys as 1/16 scale, while the Reuhl literature lists it as 1/20.*

Reuhl catalog

Left: *One of the selling points for Reuhl farm toys was that they were "a complete educational model" that could be put together and taken apart over and over again, as with this 1950s 1/16 Farmall Cub tractor. This Cub came unassembled for two dollars or assembled for three dollars, and was "constructed with real knee-action front wheels, with movable power take-off and reversible draw bar."*

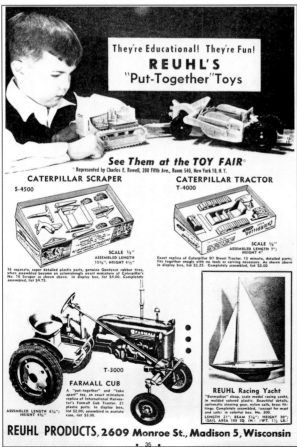

Chicago and Armstrongs in Cedar Rapids, Iowa, stores could not move the toys at Reuhl's high asking prices. In the late 1950s, the toys sold for three to four dollars at a time when dime-store toys were selling for sixty-nine cents. More than any other factor, the high prices proved to be the company's undoing.

"The life span of Reuhl Products is relatively short for a successful company," Hoover wrote. "But while his Madison plant is only a memory, the toys he produced are some of the most highly regarded and highly collected scale models ever made. This legacy probably will never disappear."

Many collectors agree with that assessment, including Gary Wandmacher of Prescott, Wisconsin. When he decided to collect farm toys, he went back and found several Reuhl toys he had as a kid: a Massey-Harris 44, a Caterpillar D7, a Caterpillar scraper, and a DW10 tractor. "I've always been attracted to the Reuhl toys," he says. "They were originally made as educational toys that you could take apart and put together again."

Marx Tin Toys

The renowned Louis Marx & Company of New York City is famous for its beautiful miniatures that are the quintessence of the American tin toy. While Marx fashioned many tin toys—including everything from clockwork cowboys swinging lariats to wind-up Mickey Mouse figures—the famous firm only made a small number of farm toys.

When he was sixteen, German immigrant Louis Marx started work at the large mechanical tin toy maker Ferdinand Strauss Corporation of New York City. By the time he was twenty, in 1916, Marx was put in charge of a toy factory in New Jersey. After a disagreement concerning manufacturing and sales philosophies, Marx parted ways with Strauss. After serving in World War I, Marx bought several old toy dies from Strauss in the early 1920s and contracted with Strauss and other toy makers to produce the toys for them bearing his own trademark.

Throughout the 1920s and 1930s, Marx built his business by buying old toy dies and subcontracting production. He eventually bought several toy factories in the United States, including in 1935, the Girard Model Works of Girard, Pennsylvania, which he renamed the Girard Manufacturing Company. He continued to produce and sell toys under both the Marx and Girard brand names. In 1928, he revived the famous Yo-Yo, and by 1950, Marx toys accounted for 12½ percent of all toys manufactured in the United States, according to Lillian Gottschalk.

Marx crawler driver
Left: *This quaint tin driver piloted Marx's crawler. Collection: Sigrid Arnott. (Photograph by Michael Dregni)*

Marx crawler advertisement
Below: *Throughout the 1920s and into the 1940s, Sears Roebuck sold tin toys manufactured by Marx in its mail-order catalog.*

Marx crawler

Marx introduced this "Reversible Six-Wheel Tractor" in 1940. The toy was detailed with features lithographed onto the tin body. The tractor was powered by a windup spring clockwork motor and boasted a reverse mechanism. The crawler measured 11¾ inches (294 mm) long. This tractor is slightly sun-faded and is missing several of its rubber wheel treads, but may still command a price of $475 in the 1990s. Collection: Sigrid Arnott. (Photograph by Michael Dregni)

Most of Marx's farm toys were not exact replicas of actual tractors, but were instead fanciful recreations of crawlers and wheeled tractors in miniature. Farm toys made by Marx include the 1926 8-inch-long (200 mm) wind-up tin American Tractor and the 1940 Aluminum Bulldog Tractor set, a wind-up tin tractor measuring 9½ inches long (237 mm).

The Marx company was sold in 1972 to the Quaker Oats Company, which also owned Fisher-Price Toys. In 1976, Marx became part of Dunbee-Combex-Marx of Europe, after which it went into bankruptcy in 1980. In 1982, American Plastics bought most of Marx's assets and began reproducing tin toys from the original Marx molds.

Buddy L Toys

Buddy L toys were named for Buddy Lundahl, the son of company founder Fred A. Lundahl. Fred founded the Moline Press Steel Company of East Moline, Illinois, in 1910, to stamp fenders and other components from 20-gauge sheet steel for International Harvester trucks. With leftover scraps, Fred fashioned dollhouse furniture for his son until Buddy's fourth birthday, in 1920, for which his father had made him a miniature version of an International truck. When all of Buddy's friends wanted one as well, Fred decided to start manufacturing stamped-steel toys.

The premiere Buddy L toys made their debut in 1921 and were such a success that the Moline Press

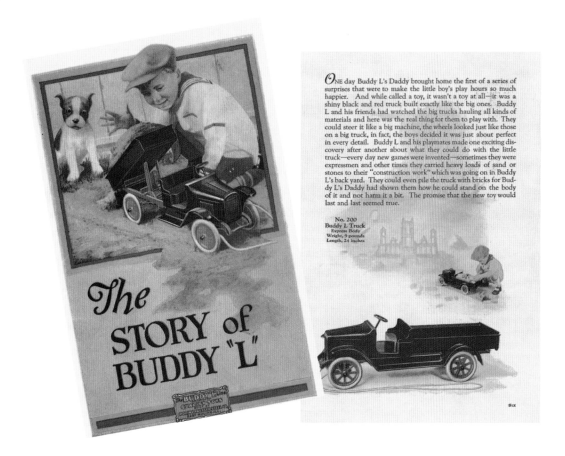

Buddy L catalog
Above, left: *This cover from a Buddy L catalog printed in 1925 shows the delight that kids get from toys, whether they are dump trucks, like this one, or other farm toys. As the catalog stated, "This is the story of Buddy L, a regular boy who found a new key to the Land of Make Believe. While all children have perhaps found Make Believe—they ride a stick and have a prancing steed—yet, Buddy L had the most fascinating toys with which he could play the kinds of games all boys dream of. These toys were real little models of big machines."*

Buddy L catalog
Above, right: *This page from the 1925 catalog shows the first Buddy L toy, the No. 200 Truck with Express body. As the text recounted, "One day Buddy L's Daddy brought home the first of a series of surprises that were to make the little boy's play hours so much happier."*

Perhaps in the strictest sense, salesman's samples are not true farm toys. But they are models of farm equipment, as are farm toys, and so many farm toy people have become fascinated with salesman's samples.

The name "salesman's samples" says exactly what these replicas are: miniature samples of farm machinery that salesmen took around the country to show farmers how different machinery worked. Collector Ken Updike of Evanston, Wisconsin, says they were used mostly during the pre–World War II era, primarily just before the turn of the century. "A salesman with a working model of a little toy reaper would hop on a train and travel from town to town, and have a kind of demo, showing people how it worked and where they could buy it, which was out of a catalog. The buyer would never see the real machine until it had been ordered and shipped to him. This was a very cost-effective way for the machinery companies to do business, instead of loading the reaper or whatever on a train and sending it around so people could see it. The salesman put the sample in his case, hopped on another train, and headed to the next town and a brand-new audience. Once the auto came around, though, I don't think the process lasted much longer."

One of toy historian Dick Sonnek's most unique toys is a salesman's sample of a Brantland-Emerson Case plow. "Probably fewer than a hundred of them were made, and were used by salesmen to take to the farm and illustrate to the farmer how this plow was

Separator salesman's sample
This wood-and-brass salesman's sample of an actual grain separator was crafted by the Northwest Thresher Company of Stillwater, Minnesota. The sample measures about 18 inches (450 mm) long, and all parts work with the turn of the miniature wheel. Collection: Washington County Historical Society. (Photograph by Michael Dregni)

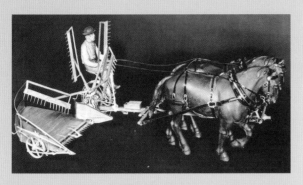

McCormick-Deering patent models
Like many agricultural companies, McCormick-Deering made models of its inventions in the early days when applying for patents. This wood model was a miniature of the McCormick-Deering Daisy reaper of 1898. Collection: State Historical Society of Wisconsin.

made. It was very lifelike, very much like the real one would be when the farmer got it sent to him on the railroad car. They were made from the 1870s through 1920 or so, and this one was made in 1910."

Sonnek also has a detailed early reaper salesman's sample, which is a little larger than the plow. As an aside he adds that cookstoves that are often called salesman's samples seldom are, but are rather detailed toys.

Salesman's samples were probably about 1/6 scale to 1/8 scale, and are highly prized and difficult to find.

Steel Company halted making full-size truck components and switched to producing miniatures. The size of most Buddy L toys was impressively large—some of the early trucks and fire engines measure up to 2 feet (600 mm) in length. They were made of the same heavy 20-gauge steel that was used for trucks and automobiles in the 1920s and were able to bear a grown person's weight.

Through the years, the company made toys under several names. Under Fred Lundahl's control, the company retained the Moline Press Steel name and merchandized its toys with the Buddy L brand name. Upon Fred's death in 1930, the firm was bought by J. W. Bettendorf and renamed the Buddy "L" Manufacturing Company. When steel was requisitioned for war materiel during World War II, Milton Klein and Henry Katz produced wooden Buddy L toys as the Buddy "L" Wood Products Company of Glen Falls, New York. Lightweight-steel Buddy L toys were manufactured in the 1950s, but the company hit hard times. In 1960, it was reorganized as the Buddy L Corporation and moved its headquarters to Neosho, Missouri, in 1969. Today, it is owned by the well-known Milton Bradley Company of Springfield, Massachusetts, which first built games and toys in 1860.

Buddy L made several farm toys over the years. The firm's first farm toy was the 1952 Pull-n-Ride Horse-Drawn Farm Wagon that measured 22¾ inches (569 mm) in length. The Buddy L Farm Combination Set of 1956 contained a cattle transport stake truck, six plastic steers, a trailer dump truck, three farm machines, and a farm machinery trailer hauler.

In 1961, Buddy L released an orange molded-plastic four-wheel Polysteel Farm Tractor that was 12 inches (300 mm) long. The Brute Farm Tractor-n-Cart followed in 1969. The Brute Tractor was bright blue with a green plastic radiator, engine, exhaust, and driver's seat, and pulled a detachable two-wheel open cart; the set measured 6¼ inches (156 mm) long. Buddy L made three editions of its 13-inch-long (325 mm) Husky tractor, in 1966, 1969, and 1970. The tractors were bright yellow with large rear fenders and black engines. The firm also made a 10½-inch-long (262-mm) Ruff-n-Tuff tractor in 1971.

Barclay Toys

The Barclay Manufacturing Company of Union City, New Jersey, was best known for its hollow-cast toy soldiers. The firm also made ambulances, army items such as anti-aircraft guns and armored trucks, along with fire engines, and racing cars. In all, Barclay made about 150 different toys in the 1930s and 1940s.

Barclay's lone claim to fame in the farm toy market was a 2⅛-inch-long (53-mm) Fordson tractor with white rubber tires and red wooden wheels.

Structo Toys

The Structo Manufacturing Company of Freeport, Illinois, has been famous for generations as the manufacturer of Erector Sets. The firm was founded by Louis and Edward Strohacker and C. C. Thompson in 1908; a dozen years later, it started making toy vehicles. Structo was bought by J. G. Cokey as majority owner in 1935. The company was later bought by the Ertl Company in 1975.

Structo's best known farm toy is its massive 1919 20-inch-long (500-mm) Yuba tractor. In 1921, the firm made a 9-inch-long (225-mm) Caterpiller miniature, followed in 1929 by a 12½-inch-long (312-mm) climbing tractor that had chain-link treads.

Dent Toys

The venerable Dent Hardware Company of Fullerton, Pennsylvania, began making toys in 1898 and is known for the particularly fine castings of its vehicles. The company was begun by Henry H. Dent and four partners and lasted until 1978.

During that time, Dent made a wide variety of cast-iron toys, including cars and trucks. Dent is revered today for its particularly fine castings. Its most famous farm toy is the rare 5¾-inch-long (143.75-mm) Fordson F tractor with only two hoods bands made during the 1930s. The Fordson boasted a separately cast, nickel-plated driver and a wide-front end.

Dent also created a cast-iron 1/16 Allis-Chalmers WC toy tractor in 1940. This was a row-crop model, with a separately cast driver and the company name cast into the toy.

Kenton Toys

The Kenton Hardware Manufacturing Company of Kenton, Ohio, began producing toys in 1903. The firm was founded in 1890 as the Kenton Lock Manufacturing Company before changing its name in 1894.

Kilgore Toys

The Kilgore Company of Westerville, Ohio, began making toys in the 1920s, most of them of cast iron and low priced. Its most popular line was cast-iron cap pistols, but it also made trucks, fire engines, cars, airplanes, and ships. Some manufacturing was done in Lancaster, Pennsylvania, and Canada. In 1937, Kilgore ventured into plastic toys, making it one of the earliest toy companies to make plastic replicas.

Kilgore's farm toys included a pair of Fordson F tractors with cast-in drivers and steel wheels. One was 4 inches (100 mm) long and rode on rubber wheels; the other was 5⅛ inches (128 mm) in length.

Kenton Fordson F
The Kenton Hardware Manufacturing Company of Kenton, Ohio, offered this cast-iron Fordson F with nickel-plated, removable driver. Collection: Ray Lacktorin. (Photograph by Michael Dregni)

Chapter 5

Modern Farm Toys

The era of the modern farm toy began with the end of World War II. With the shift away from producing war materiel, valuable wartime materials such as tin and iron were available once again to make toys. And in 1946, Fred Ertl Sr. cast his first toy, presaging the dominance of the Ertl Company, the rise of numerous other farm toy makers, and the period of the modern farm toy.

Ertl Toys: Precision Models

The Ertl Company, Inc., the giant of today's farm toy world, got its start in 1945 in the humble basement of Fred Ertl Sr.

Ertl was a molder who was unemployed due to a strike at the Dubuque, Iowa, foundry where he worked. He desperately needed an income as he had a wife and five children to support, but he was unable to find another job. Sitting around the house, he was watching his children as they played with their old Arcade toy tractors, when ten-year-old Joe broke his toy and asked his dad to fix it. When the tractor proved unrepairable, an idea was born. Fred had lots of spare time while he was without work, so he made a reproduction of the cast-iron Arcade tractor in the household furnace. He enjoyed crafting the toy tractor and realized he could do it for a living—at least until the foundry strike was over.

Fred made sand molds of several tractors. Then he melted metal in the furnace and poured it into the sand molds. After the pieces had cooled and set, his children assembled the tractors, his wife painted them, and Fred sold them. Soon afterwards, a neighbor who was a buyer for Roshek's Department Store in Dubuque saw Ertl's tractor. He examined it closely and told Fred, "I'll take all you can make." Ertl's little business thrived.

People who saw Ertl's homemade toy tractors were amazed by the quality of workmanship. Fred forgot about returning to the Dubuque foundry; he had discovered his life's work.

The business soon became a full-time project, as Fred hit the road, contacting implement dealers in the nearby towns of Dyersville, Winthrop, and Cascade about using the model tractors in their promotions. He had nothing but success: The dealers liked the toys and their customers loved them.

By 1947, the business had grown so large that it could no longer comfortably be contained in the Ertl basement. Fred moved his company to a west-side Dubuque building.

It was just the beginning. In the ensuing years, orders poured in. The growth forced Fred to make additions to the original building. Soon, this first building ran out of space, and Fred decided to build a factory.

He looked around for a good place and discovered that the Dyersville Development Corporation was looking for new businesses. The group convinced Fred that the place to build was in the eastern part of Dyersville, Iowa. Fred agreed. Construction started, and the plant was soon finished. In July 1959, production got underway in the new facility, with 16,000 square feet (1,440 sq-m) of space and fifty employees.

In 1967, the company became a subsidiary of the Victor Comptometer Corporation, assuring security and more growth for the company. It soon became evident that the firm needed other types of toys to market alongside its high-quality die-cast line. So, in January 1971, Ertl purchased Carter Tru-Scale Products, thereby enlarging its line with more farm toys.

In September 1972, Ertl struck again, adding a new line called Plastic Model Kits. In 1974, it purchased the Structo Toy Division of the King Steely Thermos Company and introduced the Structo steel toy line as an Ertl product, opening a new field in the toy market to the firm. The Structo line of steel-stamped toys was changed in 1976 to become Ertl steel-stamped miniatures, coinciding with Ertl's reputation of producing toys with precise details. As the plant expanded and the capability for producing more products increased, Ertl joined the export field. In 1973, Ertl became active in selling toys in Canada, Europe, South Africa, Australia, Japan, Singapore, Hong Kong, and elsewhere.

While Ertl originally was known for its farm toys, today its catalogs list hundreds of individual toys and

Carter Tru-Scale Farmall 560
Previous page: *Carter Tru-Scale made this 1/16 Farmall 560 tractor with a steerable narrow front end in 1960. It is hooked to a pressed-steel grain drill made in 1972.*

Ertl John Deere A

Above: *This rare Ertl 1/16 John Deere A was made in 1945 from sand-cast aluminum and rode on aluminum wheels. Made in the basement of the home of Fred Ertl Sr., it was one of Ertl's first tractors. It is worth about $1,000 in excellent condition in the 1990s. Collection: Eldon Trumm.*

Ertl Allis-Chalmers WC

Right: *This tractor is often considered the first farm toy made by Fred Ertl Sr. There are differences of opinion among knowledgeable collectors, however, who prefer to call it "one of the first." This 1/16 Allis-Chalmers WC was made of sand-cast aluminum circa 1945 in the Ertl household furnace. This example has been restored.*

Ertl Allis-Chalmers WC
This beautiful and highly detailed 1/16 Allis-Chalmers WC tractor was one of Ertl's stylish Precision Classic Series, and was die-cast in 1993.

Ertl Cockshutt 40 Black Hawk
Ertl manufactured this die-cast 1/16 Cockshutt 40 Black Hawk with crown fenders in 1988 for the National Farm Toy Museum's third series, known as the third Dyersville Museum Set.

NEW *Ertl* TRUCKS for '66

Twenty years of fine toy making . . . and dealer profit making . . . enable us to offer these superior fast selling die cast aluminum metal scale model trucks. **KEEP YOUR SALES ROLLING YEAR 'ROUND** with Ertl trucks, tractors and accessories . . . the best that skill and experience can build.

TRUCK FEATURES: All ERTL trucks are die-cast aluminum metal and have full plastic windows and interior with man, except 391. All have authentic trade mark decals, 2-toned grilles, spoked wheels with rubber tires, plastic headlights and display box. All are 1/16" scale.

No. 4800 IH LOADSTAR STAKE TRUCK. 1/16 scale model of International Loadstar Stake Truck. Removable stakes. Painted green metallic and white with silver grille.

L. 15", H. 5½", W. 6". St. Pk. 6 per 17½ lb. ctn. Suggested retail $3.50

L. 13", H. 6¼", W. 5½". St. Pk. 6 per 18¾ lb. ctn. Suggested retail $4.00.

No. 4810 IH LOADSTAR DUMP TRUCK. 1/16 scale model International Loadstar Dump Truck.

No. 4820 IH LOADSTAR DELUXE DUMP TRUCK.

Hydraulic dump with movable tail gate. Red cab and white dump box and grille.

1/16 scale model International Loadstar heavy duty dump truck with splash boards on box.

No. 4890 IH LOADSTAR FIRE TRUCK. 1/16 scale model of International Loadstar fire and rescue truck. Steel box and ladders. Red with white grille.

L. 13½", H. 5½", W. 5½". St. Pk. 6 per 15 lb. ctn. Suggested retail $4.50.

No. 4830 IH LOADSTAR TILT BED TRUCK WITH TRACTOR. 1/16"scale model International Loadstar truck with 1/16" scale model IH 404 Tractor No. 437.

L. 15", H. 7¼", W. 6". St. Pk. 6 per 24.5 lb. ctn. Suggested Retail $5.50.

Steel tilt bed deck with winch. Truck painted green metallic with white tilt bed and grille. Tractor steers with steering wheel. Painted IH red and white.

OTHER *Ertl* FARM SETS

No. 5003 DELUXE OLIVER FARM SET.
All items 1/16 metal scale models. Die cast aluminum. No. 604 Oliver tractor steers with steering wheel. Large rubber rear tires. No. 12-O steel wagon with rubber tires and movable tail gate. No. 26 die cast aluminum spreader with movable beater. No. 27 die cast aluminum 4-bottom plow with movable wheel for raising and lowering plow. No. 28 die cast zinc disc has 4 sets of plastic rollers and wheels which raise and lower for transportation or play discing. All painted Oliver green and white, with authentic decals. Packed in shrink film display-bonus box which opens up into a machine shed. L. 18¾", W. 14 1/8", H. 5¾". St. Pk. 3 per 16¾ lb. ctn. Suggested retail $10.00.

No. 5010 IH DELUXE FARM SET.
All items 1/16 metal scale models. Die cast aluminum zinc and steel. No. 435 tractor, steers with steering wheel. Large rubber rear tires. No. 438 steel and aluminum barge wagon with auto-type steering and movable tail gate. No. 442 plow with movable wheels for raising and lowering plow. No. 439 disc has four sets of plastic rollers and wheels which raise and lower for transportation or play discing. All painted IH red and white with authentic decals. Packed in shrink film display-bonus box which opens up into a machine shed. L. 16 1/8", W. 15 5/8", H.6½". St. Pk. 3 per 16 lb. ctn. Suggested retail $10.00.

No. 803 FORD DELUXE FARM SET.
All items metal scale models, die cast aluminum, zinc and steel. Consists of No. 805 Ford tractor with front wheel steering, extra large rear wheels and two toned fenders. Steel wagon with rubber tires and movable tail gate. Die cast aluminum 4-bottom plow with movable wheel for raising and lowering plow. Die cast zinc disc has four sets of plastic rollers and wheels which raise and lower for transportation or play discing. All painted Ford blue and white with authentic Ford decals. Packed in shrink film display-bonus box which opens up into a machine shed. L. 16 1/8", W.15 5/8", H. 6½". St. Pk. 3 per 17½ lb. ctn. Suggested retail $10.00.

No. 5005 IH STANDARD FARM SET.
Three piece set consists of No. 437 Farmall Tractor with steering, No. 12 steel wagon and 3-bottom plow. All painted IH red and white. Attractively packed in shrink film display box. L. 13", W. 8½", H. 4¾". St. Pk. 6 per 20 lb. ctn. Suggested retail $5.00.

No. 5011 TRACTOR WAGON SET.
Another high quality Ertl set consisting of No. 437 Tractor with steering and 3½" dia. rubber tires with IH decals and No. 12 all steel Flare Box Wagon with tail gate that opens, front wheel steering, all rubber wheels. Packed in shrink film display box. L. 18½", W. 4¼", H. 5". St. Pk. 6 per 16¼ lb. ctn. Suggested retail $3.20.

No. 5012 TRACTOR LOADER SET.
Consists of No. 408 IH tractor and No. 444 IH end loader. Tractor steers, loader raises, lowers and dumps. Tractor painted IH red and loader painted IH white with IH decals. Packed in attractive shrink film carton. L. 13", W. 5", H. 5". St. Pk. 6 per 16 lb. ctn. Suggested retail $5.00.

Ertl farm sets

Above: *By 1966, Ertl offered numerous farm sets featuring different makes of tractors.*

Ertl Fordson

Left, top: *This 1/16 Fordson was produced by Ertl in the late 1980s.*

Ertl John Deere lawn and garden tractor

Left, bottom: *Four varieties of this 1/16 John Deere 140 lawn and garden tractor with accompanying dump cart were made by Ertl in 1969. These die-cast tractors were worth about $200 in excellent condition in the late 1990s. The other tractors were painted white with red, orange, yellow, or, like this one, blue.*

model kits, including die-cast toy trucks, construction vehicles, including riding cycles and "ride-on" cars, stamped-steel toy trucks and other vehicles, die-cast miniature toys in 1/64 and 1/25 scale, plastic and die-cast model kits, Vanity Fair phonographs, radio-controlled vehicles, Discovery science toys, and more.

With thousands of trucks, tractors, and other vehicles coming off its production line daily, Ertl makes more farm tractors than any other toy farm tractor manufacturer. Ertl has grown from a tiny family enterprise to become a worldwide marketer of toys and model kits, one of the largest manufacturers of die-cast and steel toys anywhere. Ertl toys cover every spectrum of the farm toy market; some of the rarest include the 1995 Case 590 tractor, the International Harvester 3088 farm set with cows, plow, and wagon, and the scarce gold-plated 1956 John Deere 560 tractor.

In 1967, the Victor Comptometer Corporation (VCC) bought Ertl; in 1977 VCC merged with Kid, Inc., of Saddle Brook, New Jersey. In late 1988, Kid was purchased by Hanson Industries, a huge British/American venture.

"The strength of the Ertl Company," said then-President Fred Ertl Jr. in 1988, "is the skill and dedication of its people. They are people of strong moral fiber, typical of rural mid-America. They understand good work and quality products, and it is translated directly into the value and durability of our toys."

"A lot of what Ertl is will remain the same," says George Valance, recent President and CEO of the Ertl Company, "and so will what the Ertl family brought to the company, but at a slower pace."

Ertl John Deere lawn and garden tractor

Above: *This lawn and garden tractor set represents the John Deere 30 series, and was manufactured in 1/16 by Ertl in the 1970s. The die-cast trailer had a friction dump latch. The 30 series was differentiated from the 50 series by the decal on the side of the tractor: On the 30 series, the decals were a solid yellow stripe, while on the 50 series the decals were "strobed" (also known as "light bar decal") by a series of black vertical lines. Collection: State Historical Society of Wisconsin.*

Right: **1967 Ertl catalog**

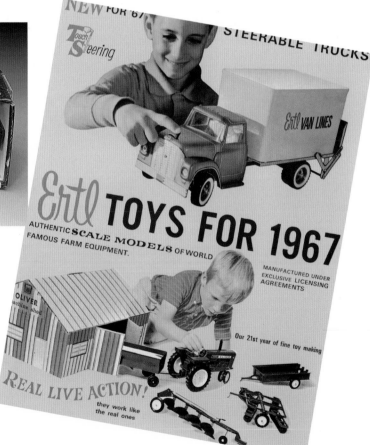

Ertl John Deere 7520
This articulated, steerable Ertl 1/16 four-wheel-drive John Deere 7520 tractor was die-cast in 1972. It is worth nearly $300 in excellent condition in the 1990s. Collection: Eldon Trumm.

Ertl International Harvester 340 Utility
Ertl made this die-cast 1/16 International Harvester 340 Utility tractor as a steerable model in 1959 with a fast-hitch. Collection: State Historical Society of Wisconsin.

Ertl Farmall Super M
A fine example of Ertl Precision Series models. Collection: Ken Updike.

Arcade John Deere A

Above: *Arcade's 1/16 John Deere A is a classic vintage collectible from the 1940s. The nickel-plated driver was removable. Collection: Ray Lacktorin. (Photograph by Michael Dregni)*

Ertl Massey-Ferguson 1155

Right: *In the 1970s, Ertl began releasing its Blueprint Replica plastic model kits, including this 1/25 Massey-Ferguson 1155.*

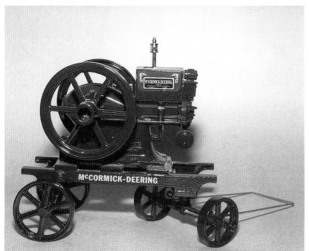

Ertl John Deere stationary engine
Above: *Ertl offered this John Deere stationary engine on a truck.*

Ertl McCormick-Deering stationary engine
Left: *Ertl offered this 1/6 Model M McCormick-Deering 1½-horsepower engine in 1990. (Photograph by Bill Vossler)*

"All right, what's in my oven this time?" Melanie Garbers of Fairmont, Minnesota, will ask her husband, Dennis, who will have to admit that it's not a soufflé, but rather a John Deere D or a Massey-Harris 44. That's the kind of thing that farm toy restorers cook up, heating the bodies of tractors they are restoring at low temperature so their new paint flows and adheres better.

Restoring farm toys—making old ones look new again—has become big business.

For many, it's the chance to make farm toys look like they did when they were kids. Collector Ordean Swain of rural Zumbrota, Minnesota, says he wanted to make his childhood toys look better. When he couldn't find anyone else to do it, he decided to do it himself, restoring the original farm toys he had puttered with as a kid. "The plastic M Farmall needed a new front end on it, a steering wheel, and stuff like that." So he just sat down and did it. And through that trial and error, his hobby of restoring toys was born.

Some collectors want farm toys restored in different forms so they might recreate the nostalgic memories of the real tractors they had on their farms. Ron Eliason of Buxton, North Dakota says, "My neighbors and other farmers are looking for me to make a complete set of the line they used on their farm. Farmers like replicas of tractors they had on the farm."

The value of restored farm toys drops in almost all cases, collector Ken Updike says. "The restorer might use the wrong wheel rivet, the wrong color of paint. That's especially true of cast iron: People who are cast iron collectors will pick a cast-iron toy with not a stitch of paint on it before they pick up a repainted one, because originality is big with them."

Updike says restoring and customizing modern farm toys is pretty much a way of life for those who can't afford a toy that is in mint condition or NIB— "new in box." "Then repainting might be the way to go. Some people collect brand new original farm toys, but some are glad to have it whether it is new or not. If it looks good, it serves the same purpose in the collection."

Although restored farm toys often are not as valuable as unrestored toys, people persist in restoring them. There are many reasons.

Sometimes it's just to get an old toy to look nice again so the kids can beat it up again, as restorer Francis Nicholls discovered. Two kids came to have their broken and beat-up tractors fixed. Their father said they would have to use their own money, and they had agreed. "After I restored them and they picked them up, the younger kid saw that his had a cab, while his older brother's didn't have a cab, so the older brother could put the tractor on the floor and turn the steering wheel. The younger kid kept looking at his brother's toy, and his dad said 'What's wrong?' He said he didn't want a cab on his, and this was after I'd spent all that time making that cab perfect."

Francis obliged the boy and cut the cab off. "The kid was happier than heck," he says. "He could turn the steering wheel now."

A year later, Francis ran into the same two kids at a fair. They had their tractors with them, as broken and beat up as if they had never been restored. "Be darned if they didn't want me to fix them again," he says. "This time I reinforced them. They had been so proud of those tractors when they walked out with them a year before, and when they brought them back, they were disasters."

Some people restore farm toys because they enjoy the challenge. Eliason says he likes stuff that is pure junk, all beat up so he can redo it and make it perfect. "I like to make it look as much like the original as possible, but only if that's what the customer wants."

"The hardest part is seeing that the paint doesn't run or chip. I've painted some tractors three times before I've given them to the customer. I try to make them perfect. The tougher the shape they are in when I get them, the better I like it." He says he constantly refers to books to make sure he's doing it right. "Without the books, it would be tough."

He says he never gets tired of it. "Sometimes I'll still be working at 2 A.M., realizing how much I enjoy it."

Some collectors want restored toys because they're

more affordable than those unrestored toys in better condition. Nicholls wanted toys from the 1960s and 1970s. He quickly figured it would be cheaper to buy a junker and fix it than to buy one in better condition. "I painted and redid and customized some of my own instead of buying," he says, "and I saved a lot of money."

Others began restoring because parts to fix broken tractors weren't available. Dennis Garbers says that was how he got into restoration in 1976. For him, necessity was the mother of invention. "There were no wheels, no decals, no mufflers either. You had to make do with what you had, or else you built it."

The hardest farm toys to restore are the implements that have been bent up, Nicholls says. "You have to unbend them, or make a part, to restore them to how they looked originally. That's the hardest part. You have to see in your mind what it's going to look like when it's done. You have to visualize it. That makes the job easier." Otherwise, he says, you can stumble into dead ends.

Working on 1/64 tractors is a problem too, Nicholls says. "Because of all the time you put into it, you can't charge what you really need. And people who look at it don't think it's worth what you're charging, because the toy is so small."

For Garbers, cast iron is the toughest to restore. "When you put something back together, it's supposed to be refinished. But the casts were rough back then, and you try to make the finished product look like it's thirty or forty years old. Cast iron doesn't look right when it's shiny. It must be dulled or aged somewhat."

When restoring for others, Eliason bids first on the piece and tells the collector exactly what it will cost before he touches it. "I want the customer to be satisfied and me to be satisfied. I examine the tractor, and itemize everything so it's all clear. Most people give me the tractor to work on after I've bid on it. If I find during fixing it that something was hidden and it will cost more, I'll call the person back and tell them, and ask them if they want me to fix it. One man didn't, but then he called back two days later and changed his mind."

The process of restoration generally goes like this: First, the toy is disassembled, and the tires are removed; taking off the tires is often one of the most difficult parts, but soaking them in hot water helps. Next, the broken parts that can be fixed are repaired. Eliason says he drills and pins everything. "I use wire, liquid steel, JB weld. And if I have to, I make something out of nothing. I try to make parts at times if it's something I can't get from one of the parts dealers—and that isn't much. You can restore old broken toys nowadays that would have been thrown out just a few years ago."

Then, the paint is removed with a glass bead blaster or by other methods. Garbers says his glass beader "blows ground up glass at 80–85 pounds pressure. I prefer glass because sand is more gritty and harsh." He added that when he sands the body, he uses plastic gloves. "I try to keep the fingerprints off."

Next, the body is patched with JB weld, and then it is let set for twenty-four hours. After the weld has dried, the toy is baked in the oven for forty-five minutes to an hour at 140°Fahrenheit (60°Celsius).

After the tractor has cooled, it is painted. Because painting is so difficult, some restorers, like Garbers, subcontract it. Eliason uses spray paint, "cans of implement paint from John Deere or IH or wherever." He's learned that different colors and brands of paint react differently applied, and he has to be aware of that as he's painting. "Some are thicker and some are thinner, for instance," he says.

After the tractor has been painted, the tires are mounted on the rims once more, and the front wheels are riveted onto new axles.

The final touch is to put the decals on the tractor, if needed. Restorer Gene Birklid of Nome, North Dakota, says "The most aggravating part is putting decals on. It takes just one second to ruin them."

"Then I let it set all night," Garbers says. "The next day I wipe it down to get rid of the fingerprints, and it's ready to go on the shelf. I'm pretty fussy. It's brand new when it's done. I like to compare how it looked before, and then compare it with the finished product."

Eska Toys

The Eska Company began as a shipping firm to distribute farm toys. Eska was an early player in the farm toy field, formed as a middleman company after a meeting in late 1945 between Fred Ertl Sr., Eldon "Bud" Session, and Lavern D. Kasei. Eska's name was created from the first two letters of Session's and Kasei's last names.

The three men wanted to provide Ertl farm toys, with the original equipment manufacturer's (OEM) logo—John Deere, International Harvester, or whatever—to the OEM company. Under the agreement, Ertl products were delivered to Eska, which shipped them to Deere dealerships throughout the United States. One other agreement was made clear: Ertl made tractors, and Eska, or later, Carter Tru-Scale, would make implements. Eska did not manufacture tractors.

This arrangement continued until 1948, when Eska began making steel-stamped farm implements in its building at Thirty-second and White Streets in Dubuque, Iowa. "Carter Tru-Scale made the tools and designed the product," Fred Ertl Jr. says—although the Carter name never appeared on the product or boxes.

In 1950–1951, Eska's debt outran the company's assets, and Carter Tru-Scale took over the Eska manufacturing operation, moving it to Rockford, Illinois, where Carter Tru-Scale's stamping operation was located. The acquisition of Eska gave Carter Tru-Scale the ability to expand its farm toy production. Carter crafted toys under both the Carter Tru-Scale, and Eska brand names.

The early 1/16 Eska implements included a pair of International Harvester manure spreaders made in 1950 and 1956; a loader for Farmall 400 and 450 tractors made in 1955; and a hard-to-find set with a Farmall M tractor, spreader, and plow produced in 1950.

Eska gained another product line when Fred Ertl Sr. discontinued production of the few large sand-cast riding, or pedal, tractors he had built. Eska took over production, and it is today best remembered for its pedal tractors. Eska made various types of John Deere pedal tractors and accompanying Deere trailers. The first sand castings were made at several places in Wisconsin and Minnesota, while the final assembly was done at Eska. Eska also made cardboard farm buildings in 1950.

In late 1959, Eska and Ertl went their separate ways, and in 1960–1961, Ertl obtained Eska's licensing rights for Deere, International Harvester, Case, Oliver, and Allis-Chalmers.

Some Eska farm toys included an Allis-Chalmers trailer in 1950 and 1960, a Case tractor umbrella, Oliver 2-wheel trailers in 1950 and 1960, and others.

Eska pedal tractors included a series of International Harvester Farmall H and Farmall M pedal tractors from 1949 to 1955, among many others.

Eska established other business sidelines, including the manufacture of lawn mowers, exercise bicycles, and, eventually, outboard motors, but went out of business in 1986.

Eska International Harvester plow

This Eska 1/16 International Harvester two-bottom plow was made of pressed steel in the 1950s. It contained several variations in the colors of the wheels, and one variation in which the rear wheel is of solid rubber, unlike this example. Collection: State Historical Society of Wisconsin.

Eska John Deere baler
Above: *Eska produced this 1/16 John Deere 14-T baler in 1952 from pressed steel. It contained metal teeth in the hay pickup, and was almost exactly like one Eska made six years later that had plastic teeth in the pickup and came with or without a hitch on the side of the bale chamber.*

Eska Case farm wagon
Left: *In the 1950s, Joe Carter designed this tin 1/16 Case flare-box grain wagon for the Eska Company of Dubuque, Iowa. The wheels were made of rubber, while the rims were tin. Many of the Carter-made Eska farm toys were variously called Carter or Eska toys. Collection: State Historical Society of Wisconsin.*

Ertl Farmall 560 with Eska loader

Above: *This Ertl 1/16 Farmall 560 tractor was fitted with a 1/16 International Harvester loader crafted by Eska in 1960. The loader was made from pressed steel to fit Ertl's Farmall 560 or 460. Collection: State Historical Society of Wisconsin.*

Eska International Harvester manure spreader

Right: *Eska manufactured this 1/16 International Harvester manure spreader from pressed steel in 1956. Collection: State Historical Society of Wisconsin.*

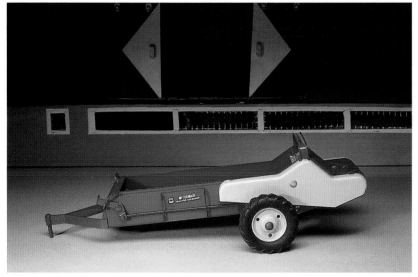

Carter made this Tru-Toy farm set of a 1/32 Farmall M with four implements—a disc, plow, drag, and spreader, along with eight animals—in 1948. It is worth about $500 in the 1990s.

Carter and Carter Tru-Scale Toys

Most people think of Carter Tru-Scale as a single farm toy manufacturer, but in that thinking they are only half correct. At first, Carter did not manufacture farm toys at all, but the firm later expanded into farm toys, releasing toys under both the Carter, and then Carter Tru-Scale, names.

In 1946, Carter Machine and Tool Company was a parts maker, supplying stamped-steel toy implements components under contract to the Eska Company. Eska assembled and painted the wagons, plows, and manure spreaders, selling them first to John Deere and, eventually, to International Harvester. Although Carter founder Joe Carter innovated and designed many of the parts, his name never appeared on the Eska toys. In 1950–1951, Eska defaulted on its debts to Carter, and in 1951, Eska was turned over to Joe Carter in payment.

Starting in 1950, Carter made several farm toys bearing his name, including an International Harvester two-bottom plow in 1950 and a John Deere 1/16 pressed-steel manure spreader with rubber tires. Also in 1950, Carter began making the highly respected and crafted Tru-Scale farm toys, also known as Carter Tru-Scale farm toys. Among the first Tru-Scale toys was the 1950 M and 860 tractors, as well as combines, discs, elevators, plows, and trailers. Modern collectors identify these Carter Tru-Scale toys with fine crafts-

manship, but they often do not realize that Carter's fine work is also found in Eska's farm implements, including its wagons, spreaders, drills, and balers. All of these were Carter's creations even though his name did not appear on any of the toys.

Carter's reputation for building faithful replicas was illustrated by his son-in-law, George Anderson. When Anderson came to work at Carter in 1952, Joe Carter handed him a Deere catalog for a corn picker and told him to measure every part of the real picker on an implement dealer's lot, and then make a miniature one. With those measurements in hand, Anderson learned how to make the 1/16 toy as he went, crafting the easiest parts first. Anderson still owns that prototype Deere picker he made in 1952.

In the mid-1950s, Carter Tru-Scale had a chance to make a huge expansion by selling toys in volume to K-Mart. But Joe Carter chose not to expand. He wanted to take time with the projects rather than be held accountable to producing toys for someone else. In 1971, Carter Machine and Tool Company was sold to Victor Comptometer, which was by then also the parent company of Ertl.

Like many of the best farm toy makers, Joe Carter created farm toys not for fame or fortune, but to make the best and most realistic replicas that he could. Carter's steel implements were the first of their kind, and today continue to be among the most desirable farm toys in the hobby.

Carter Tru-Scale Farmall M
Carter Tru-Scale manufactured this Tru-Scale 1/16 Farmall M tractor in the early 1950s with a swivel front. The Tru-Scale loader is typical of those made by Carter. Other versions of this pressed-steel loader were made to fit particular tractor models and were manufactured by Eska with "McCormick" decals on the sides. The short-style loader was made to fit a Farmall 400 or 450, while the long-style loader fit a Farmall 560.

Spec-Cast Toys

In 1974, Phil Robinson started the Spec-Cast Company in Rockford, Illinois, to produce and sell centrifugal-cast-made belt buckles. "Running Spec-Cast was fun," Robinson said in a 1989 interview. "I enjoyed the creativity and the freedom. I have no regrets. I got to do what I wanted to do and, at the same time, serve a public that was looking for our products." Spec-Cast soon expanded into making placards, desk pen sets, and trophy-type items.

In 1977, the firm was sold to Doug Klarman and Don Howell, both of whom had been involved in the industry for two decades. They chose their leadership positions scientifically: with a coin flip. Howell won president, Klarman vice-president.

Spec-Cast had not been delivering products on time when the duo took over the company, Klarman

says. But they got a quick introduction into the common etiquette of farm industry people. "International Harvester was our biggest customer at that time," Klarman remembers. "They called with a huge special order and said they would pay us some in advance if we needed the money to buy the lead. You don't find stuff like that often in industry—any industry." At that time, the replicas they made consisted of mobile cranes and trenching equipment, among others.

In 1979, Spec-Cast was bought by Ernie Jackson, who had worked at Ertl in charge of farm toys. Jackson intended to diversify out of the company's reliance on belt buckle production, which comprised 95 percent of the line. Jackson also thought more work needed to be done developing products at the start. In that way, he said in a 1989 interview, "You cut down on how much time you spend reworking each of the

Spec-Cast Case DC
This die-cast 1/16 Case DC tractor was made by Spec-Cast of Dyersville, Iowa, in the mid-1990s.

pieces that comes out of the cast. That's how we built the business. Work up front, instead of later."

In 1986, Spec-Cast was sold to Dave Bell, who had been in charge of farm toys at Ertl. As Jackson remembered the deal, "For four years, every time I saw [Bell], he asked if I wanted to sell [Spec-Cast]. One day he asked me to name a price. I did, and in 1986, he and his brother, Ken, bought it. Today I wonder why I sold the business."

After years of marketing, licensing, and developing products for the replica industry, buying Spec-Cast fed right into Dave Bell's strengths. "It was just a natural progression, a next logical step," he says. "This business fits what I know most about. I'm just in a different building."

The Bell brothers wanted to diversify further, moving into farm toy collectibles in 1986. They grew the company rapidly, moving it from Rockford to Dyersville, Iowa.

Today, Spec-Cast produces 1/43 pewter tractors

Spec-Cast Allis-Chalmers A
Spec-Cast manufactured this 1/16 Allis-Chalmers A tractor on rubber in the 1990s.

as collector items. Dave Bell explains: "A lot of these are done for individuals, on contract, usually collectors who couldn't find a particular tractor and decided to have a number of them made. They usually sell off most of the run to cover costs." Spec-Cast also continues to sell belt buckles and other specialty items, with Dave Bell as president and Ken Bell as vice-president. Some of Spec-Cast's farm toys include a zinc Fairbanks-Morse engine made for B&B Buckles; a John Deere Froehlich tractor made of pewter in 1993; a First Edition Fiat G240 tractor made of die-cast steel in 1994; and many others.

Scale Models

Although Scale Models did not become a company until 1977, its roots wander back thirty-two years to the basement of Fred Ertl's house in Dubuque, Iowa, in 1945, and the scene that also gave birth to the Ertl Company. Ten-year-old Joe Ertl's beloved Arcade toy tractor that broke and sparked his father to begin sand-casting reproductions in the household furnace also sparked Joe's interest. Joe grew up in the toy business: He assembled and painted toy tractors in his early years, and then learned to market, design, and engineer the Ertl Company's "blueprint replica" toys. As early as 1953, when Joe was still in high school, he was also working for his father's business in his spare time and designed many of the early Ertl replicas.

The family business became a subsidiary of the Victor Comptometer Corporation in 1967, and soon Joe began to think about establishing another, purely family-owned business. In 1970, the thirty-five-year-old Joe created Dyersville Die Casting. "I didn't like the bureaucracy of a big corporation," Joe said in a 1989 interview. "Either I had to do something now or stay here at Ertl forever."

Dyersville Die Casting was housed in a 10,000-square-foot (900-sq-m) building and started with ten workers who produced zinc and aluminum die-cast parts according to the customer's specifications. The company also machined and assembled the castings it produced for electrical appliances, farm equipment, automotive and office equipment, electrical instruments and fittings, furniture, outdoor products, and hydraulic equipment. The fledgling firm grew slowly. As Joe said, "I don't like to go too fast at any one point."

In 1977, White Farm Equipment approached Joe Ertl about making model tractors for the company. Joe mulled the offer over—taking time, as was his trademark—and decided that returning to his roots and making farm toys was what he would like to do. Scale Models was born in 1978.

From that single contract, Scale Models has grown rapidly until it now handles more than a hundred different projects, from pedal tractors to toy tractors, model car kits to novelty items like belt buckles and sculptures. It employs more than 110 workers in five different plants, and continues to grow. And Scale Models remains the family business Joe wanted, with his three children and two sons-in-law working for him.

Through the years, Joe showed his business cau-

Scale Models
John Deere A
Both photos: *Scale Models's new 1/8 farm toys featured great detail at a relatively inexpensive price. This 1/8 John Deere A was one of six replicas introduced by Scale Models in the 1990s.*

Scale Models range

Above: *A selection from Scale Models's vast range of different replicas in different scales.*

Scale Models catalog

Left: *Scale Models makes all different sizes of farm toys, including these 1/16 tractors, including an Oliver 70 and 1855, and a Minneapolis-Moline UDLX and G940.*

tion and acumen. In the late 1980s, he was asked to expand Scale Models to make a huge number of toys for a major company. But Joe liked his business small, and his prudence proved a godsend when the major company got in financial trouble just a few years later. Had Scale Models expanded, they too would have been in deep financial trouble.

The toy business, Joe Ertl said, has provided him with good fun and good friends. "Plus, you're creating something for kids. You think, 'Some kid will enjoy this.'

"I have no desires to become a huge corporation," Joe said. "Nor do I have any desire to sell. What we're doing here is more than just making something to make a buck."

Among many others, Scale Models products included a Collector Series of Massey-Harris General Purpose four-wheel drive, Fordson N, Huber L, Twin City 17/28, and "Green" D, as unlicensed models are termed following the real manufacturer's tractor paint scheme; a Collector II Series of Green G and Oliver

80 diesel with rear spoke wheels or rear rubber tires; an Antique Series; Thresher Series; 1/32 Antique Models; 1/64 models; a J. I. Case line; Specialties, such as a 1/64 steam engine, separator, and Minneapolis-Moline UDLX Comforttractor; and items like Case Eagle plaques, model school busses, and more. One of Scale Models's latest and most innovative products included the new 1/8 series of tractors, so far consisting of a Farmall M, Farmall 560, Allis-Chalmers WD-45, and John Deere Model B.

"We didn't start with a whole lot," Joe said. "Everybody pitched in and helped. We could see it was a good thing. The move turned out to be the best thing I've ever done."

For a while, Scale Models had a museum of some 550 toy tractors and farm and industrial equipment from Joe Ertl's collection. "Some of those toys were played with by our children over the years. My boy, Don, used to pretend he was an implement dealer," Joe remembered.

Scale Models catalog
Scale Models has become well-known for its detailed, 1/16 tractors, as in this brochure picturing the Massey-Harris 44, Farmall 806, and John Deere 70.

Slik Oliver 880
Slik's 1/32 Oliver 880 tractor was often called a "dimestore model" as it was sold originally sold in the dimestores of the 1960s. It was made of sand-cast aluminum in 1960.

Tootsietoys

The roots of Tootsietoy stretch back to 1876 and Dowst & Company, publishers of the *National Laundry Journal* magazine. Samuel Dowst began making die-cast novelties and toys after buying a Linotype machine at the 1893 World's Fair. Dowst registered the Tootsietoy name in 1924.

In 1926, Dowst's company was sold to Nathan Shure, who merged it into the Cosmo Toy and Novelty Company. The Tootsietoy name appeared on a variety of toy semi-trailer tractors, tanks, buses, fire engines, and many cars. The company made several farm toys, including several different varieties of a red 1/32 8N Ford tractor with a loader during the 1950s; an International tractor; and another tractor simply called a "Farm Tractor," with a driver.

In 1961, Cosmo Toy and Novelty Company bought Strombecker Plastic Company of Rock Island, Illinois, and took on the Strombecker name.

Slik-Toys

Slik-Toys were manufactured by Slik-Toys of Lansing, Iowa, and sometimes have trademarks of "Lansing" or "Kipp" in addition to the Slik-Toy brand name.

Slik manufactured farm toys in the 1940s and 1950s. The firm crafted a series of Oliver farm miniatures, including a 1/16 pressed-steel two-row mounted corn-picker in 1948, and a sand-cast aluminum 1/16 grain drill in 1950. Slik also made a 6½-inch-long

Slik Oliver 77

Slik made this 1/16 Oliver 77 Row Crop tractor in 1952. It was one of four die-cast Oliver 77 models that Slik made in 1948 and 1952 in different variations. This one has an open engine and green wheels, while the pair of Oliver 77s made in 1948 both have drivers, one brown and one silver. The 1952 models were available with variations in the decals. This steerable model shown here is the most valuable of the four, worth about $800 in the 1990s, while the others are worth half to three quarters that.

(162-mm) die-cast International Harvester M in the 1950s. Slik also made cars, pickup trucks, fire trucks, vans, and wreckers.

Lakone Toys

Lakone-Classic of Aurora, Illinois, made farm toys in the early 1950s, including plastic 1/16 International Harvester C, IH 200, and IH 230 tractors.

The Toy Factory

The Toy Factory of Dyersville, Iowa, was a short-lived company that started in 1996. It made a 1/8 hay wagon that included real hay bales tied by hand. The company also made a 1/8 manure spreader, but sales were not good, and the company disappeared the same year it started.

Franklin Mint Precision Models

The Franklin Mint of Franklin, Pennsylvania, has become well known for its quality collectible cars, dolls, and other replicas. The firm has recently begun making farm toys, its first being a 1/12 American Legend Series Farmall H tractor, similar to the Ertl Precision Series H, but larger.

Collector Ken Updike is impressed by the first Franklin Mint Farmall. He says, "You can take the hood off and see the engine, and it has a lot more moving parts than the Ertl version. All the pedals move, the throttle lever moves and moves the linkage, the seat goes up and down like in the real tractor, and it has a real wood belt pulley like the real tractor. They can do more in a larger scale like that." He noted that the toy has a few mistakes, which were minimal and hadn't been corrected yet.

Franklin Mint Farmall H
The Franklin Mint of Franklin, Pennsylvania, released its first farm tractor replica in 1998, a 1/12 American Legend Series Farmall H, with the help of tractor historian Robert N. Pripps. (Photography by the Franklin Mint Precision Models)

New Collecting Afoot: Pedal Tractors

If farm toys can be small and operated by hand in a sandbox, why, conversely, couldn't they also be large, functional, and operated by foot? That is the premise behind pedal toys, which are roughly 1/3 to 1/5 scale of real tractors, although no actual scale corresponds to pedal tractors.

Elmer Duellman of Fountain City, Wisconsin, has more than a hundred pedal tractors—as well as hundreds of other pedal toys, including airplanes, trucks, and 500 different pedal cars. In fact, he so enjoys pedal vehicles that he was instrumental in publishing a book on them, *The Evolution of the Pedal Car*, in four volumes. Most of his pedal tractors are pictured and listed in the last volume, with a few pages of his pedal vehicles in each of the other three books.

"I started collecting pedal tractors in 1984," Duellman says. "My dad had a farm one time, and I used to work on a farm, and I think the pedal tractors are just very unique. I had a big display of them at Farm Fest recently. I took one of each kind over there, a Massey-Harris, a Case, an Allis, a Ford, an IH, an Oliver, plus some pedal trucks."

He says people really love them. "In fact, a lot of people ask me if they might not be for sale. I've got some duplicates, but I don't want to get rid of them unless I trade for something that I don't have."

Like most farm toy collectors, pedal tractor enthusiasts are a touch monomaniacal in getting their next toy. "One time a guy from Iowa called to say he had a pedal tractor I wanted, and I told him I'd be there at 8 A.M. the next morning. When I got up the next morning, gosh, there was a blizzard. But I went anyway. I did manage to get down there, where I ended up buying a one-owner CA Allis."

The John Deere A pedal tractor was one of the hardest for Elmer to find. "I'd been advertising for pedal tractors for years with a sign in my salvage business. One day a young lad came in and said he knew where there was one of them, only forty miles from here. That was an original-owner one too."

He found the rarest Ford pedal tractor, a 901 Ford with bar and grille, right in Winona, Minnesota. "I like all the little pedal tractors, the CA Allis, the Case VAC, the little Oliver. Whenever I take my pedal tractors and put them on display, those are the ones I take. They're so cute."

A few years ago, Elmer had some of his pedal tractors restored. A couple of the tractors, in their bright new shiny coats, sit on shelves in his garage.

Nowadays, he does not restore pedal tractors any more. "I think they look better if they have even just fifty percent of the original paint. That means they're child-worn, and that means the kids were having fun with them." He occasionally allows kids who come to his museum ride to them around the yard. "I just love it."

Jerry Heim of St. Joseph, Minnesota, has twenty-five pedal tractors in his collection. "I got the first one at an auction sale when I bought a junk pile, and it happened to be in there, broken in half. That was a challenge. I figured I'd see if I could fix it. So I found out where I could get parts, and found a way of welding it and restoring it, and brought it back to life again. That's my John Deere LGT."

Jerry owns a rare Sears pedal tractor. "I picked that up at a steam show. Most of those are in the rock pile, and Sears doesn't make them any more."

Once farm toy people start grabbing up pedal tractors, their interest in larger-scale farm toys increases, as Mark and Paul Brunner of Verona, Wisconsin, know. When they were kids, their mom backed the family car over their Oliver 880 pedal tractor. "We figured that ended that tractor," Paul says. "She destroyed it pretty good."

Paul says he decided to restore that Oliver 880. "After it was done, it looked really nice. That kind of got us started in making 1/5-size farm implements."

In the first year, Tom says they made a wagon, then a disk, elevator, auger, spreader, and bale rack. "Then we got more interested. We made a plow and went to more elaborate ones, like the combine, round baler that runs, sprayer, rake, blower, and right now I'm working on a hay loader, one of those from years ago that had the bars that pushed the hay up onto the wagon—'push loaders' they called them."

Their father, Tom, says he tries to find a real machine for a pattern. "I'll pick up a machine at a sale or

Pedal tractors

Nicholas (background) and Thomas Hunt of Dyersville, Iowa, have a good time riding John Deere 50 Series and Case International pedal tractors.

ask people who have them. I've borrowed a few of them. Last year my boys made a chisel plow, and a guy who had it here at the welding shop left it a little longer for us because he didn't need it, so we used that as a pattern for the 1/5-size chisel plow." They've also made a grain drill, dump rake, and feeder wagon.

They continue to restore pedal tractors for other people. "We did one for a guy just before Christmas. It belonged to him when he was a kid, and he wanted it restored for his own kid. After he saw how we'd restored it, he didn't know if he wanted to give it to his kid. He said it looked too good."

They've customized several of the pedal tractors for local pedal pull contests. "We made sleds for three of them. We customized them, put a wide front end on them, a three-point hitch, and a sunroof on one,

and a little backhoe on one, to make them more realistic, and make them look nicer, we think." A couple have weight racks on the front of them.

As more people get interested in them, pedal tractor have become harder to find. However, that doesn't stop those who really love them from trying to track them down. In fact, it probably makes them more determined. Ken Updike says that since day one almost all pedal tractors used the same-sized tires, rims, fronts, backs, steering wheels, and pedals. "The basic bodies have changed, but 85–90 percent of all pedal tractors made during the last thirty years have all those in common for sure."

Pedal tractors are manufactured by Ertl and Scale Models, and Eska was a big builder of pedal tractors in the past.

Chapter 6

Farm Toy Scratchbuilders

More than in any other field of toy collecting, farm toys are often built from scratch by collectors. Numerous specialized "scratchbuilders" craft tractors, implements, trucks, and farm buildings from raw materials. Almost all parts and components are made by hand, with the exception of tires and decals, the occasional gear in working models that needs perfect machining, or boiler parts that need to hold pressure in steam tractor models.

Many farm toy collectors are farmers, and the very nature of farm work means lulls during which farmers might have time to make different toys. Many farmers also have honed their hand-working skills after years of regular or emergency repair of real farm machinery; these skills lend themselves to fabricating farm toys.

Farm toys are scratchbuilt for many reasons. Some scratchbuilders seek to add greater detail than on many mass-produced toys; collectors want to see the toy, which often represents an actual machine they worked on, resemble the real one as closely as possible. Other scratchbuilders desire to make replicas of tractor that mainstream toy companies have never made as farm toys.

Scratchbuilt farm toys have been made for many years. One of the earliest was depicted in *Farm Implements* magazine in 1917: "Master Theodore Helbling of Gridley, Ill., enjoys the distinction of being one of the most progressive boys in his town. One of the latest results of his progressiveness and alertness has been to design and manufacture a miniature Avery tractor. This tractor is an exact replica of the big 40-80 H.P. Avery machine and it contains many of the selling points incorporated in a regular 'sure enough' Avery tractor.

"As can readily be seen by the picture, the machine has the exact design of an Avery 40-80, incorporating the sliding frame, the simple power plant, the vertical tube radiator, the cab and the big drive wheels. This little tractor will not only do traction work but it will do belt work as well, and the motor is operated by means of three dry cells, which the tractor carries behind in a little cart manufactured for the purpose.

Bob Gray Farmall F-30
Previous page: *Scratchbuilder Bob Gray of Eldora, Iowa, crafted this 1/16 Farmall F-30 from korloy in 1969.*

Frank Hansen John Deere Dain

Frank Hansen scratchbuilt 1,000 1/16 Dain tractor replicas from pressed steel in 1982. The Dain is considered the first John Deere production tractor. Surprisingly, the Hansen Dains are worth about $500 each in the 1990s, unlike some other short-run tractors that are worth much less.

Lyle Dingman John Deere D

Above: *Lyle Dingman of Spencer, Iowa, made this 1/16 John Deere Styled D tractor in 1989. Dingman made several varieties of the D over the years. Collection: Eldon Trumm.*

Lyle and Joyce Dingman

Right: *The late Lyle Dingman scratchbuilt and customized many types of farm toys. He quit a well-paying job to go into manufacturing farm toys. Some of his patterns were made by Gilson Rieke of Ruthven, Iowa, another scratchbuilder. He is pictured here with his wife Joyce in a 1989 photo. (Photograph by Bill Vossler)*

"When asked how he got the idea, the youthful designer replied that he had been looking through the Avery catalog and he thought possibly he could make up a little tractor that would run by electricity, so he went ahead and did so. He went on to say that just as soon as he grew up he wanted to study engineering, and if possible, he was going to be a designing engineer of the Avery Company some day."

Modern Scratchbuilders

Modern scratchbuilding of farm toys began when collectors could not find the toys they wanted and decided to build their own. Today, it is an integral part of the farm toy world.

The range of scratchbuilt farm toys runs the gamut. Kermit Ehrenberg of Appleton, Minnesota, for instance, has made from scratch three 1/4-size farm tractors: a 1937 F-20 Farmall, a 1938 G John Deere, and 1934 Allis-Chalmers. He decided to do his tractors in as large as scale as his lathe could allow, which meant one-quarter of the original size. So every day for ten years during the frigid Minnesota winters, he traipsed from his warm workshop into the unheated machine shed that surrounds it where he measured every bolt, nut, angle, and length of each full-sized tractor. "You draw a little blueprint on a little piece of scratch paper and then go back inside the shop and work as far as you made the blueprint, and then go back and measure again," Ehrenberg says.

Like those farm boys of years past, Kermit made do with what he could find in the farm scrap heap. "I used well casings for the back wheels, and iron I picked out of the scrap pile, or somebody else's scrap pile."

One of the oddest parts is the differential on the F-20, which is part of an oxygen tank cap. That hollow part allowed him to help keep the finished product light.

Scratchbuilders are often dedicated, even monomaniacal. It took Ehrenberg three years and 1,500 or so hours of work to craft each scratchbuilt tractor. The tractors are also detailed: Each one has functional steering, brakes, and levers, like the real tractors.

He says one of the keys to making the tractors is learning that you have to leave enough material so you can machine it down to size, rather than be short and have to do something else to correct that.

Some of the most fun is to finally get a part completed, put together, and see it fit after struggling with it for a while. "It's a good feeling rather than having a bummer or an 'oops'. There's a lot of 'oops' in this work. You break a tap off, or something, to get it out. You're working with some pretty fine threads, 40 per inch, and the taps are quite delicate. You don't dare sneeze while you're tapping threads," Ehrenberg says.

Al and Cathy Van Kley of Ankeny, Iowa, work at the other spectrum of scratchbuilding, creating 1/64 rear-mount cultivators. Al Van Kley figures they have made and sold thousands of them, working mostly on weekends with family and neighbor kids.

People who see scratchbuilt toys are often astonished that they are not factory-made. Gary Van Hove of Pipestone, Minnesota, says people constantly ask, "You built this?" and can't figure out how he did it. "They can't believe someone can take a piece of brass and make a toy out of it. There are a lot of questions: 'How do you do this?' and 'How do you put this together?'"

Gary Van Hove and his son, Chad, have built seventy different pieces of farm machinery. "Our grain truck seems to be as popular as anything, although some of the smaller things, like scraper blades for tractors, are popular," Gary Van Hove says. They also make shares, plows, and even farm animals.

In addition, they fabricate one-of-a-kind scratchbuilt items custom ordered by collectors, although Gary Van Hove says he likes to make a second one to show what he's done. All of the parts are hand crafted, hand bent, and no two pieces are alike. "I make a lot of changes while I'm working. If I form a piece, and it doesn't look right, I'll go back and redraw it. With brass you can solder, recut, and resolder."

He says the key to making great-looking scratch pieces is the paint job. "If the paint job is done right, you know the toy is done right."

One of the fascinating aspects of scratchbuilt toys is that their history is often a mystery, as with a wooden tractor Don Gross of Albert Lea, Minnesota, bought from a Wisconsin furniture dealer. "[The dealer] had some nice furniture, and setting on top of one of the tables was this tractor," Gross remembers. "I saw that thing and went back and forth and finally asked him how much he wanted. I think he asked for thirty-five dollars. It was a lot of money, but eventually I went back and bought it, because I liked it and it appealed to me.

"I think it's one of a kind. It's all wood, with rear

Charles Cox Waterloo Boy
Above: *Charles Cox of Waterloo, Iowa, scratchbuilt only nineteen of these finely detailed 1/16 Waterloo Boy tractors from sand-cast aluminum in 1973.*

Martin Fast Big Bud 500
Right: *Scratchbuilder Martin Fast created this 1/16 Big Bud 500 with a Kamatsu engine. Fast built the tractor in 1994 from sand-cast aluminum. Collection: Eldon Trumm.*

Roger Mohr Minneapolis-Moline 5-Star

Roger Mohr of Vail, Iowa, scratchbuilt this 1/16 resin model of a Minneapolis-Moline 5-Star in 1985. Mohr made several variations of the tractor: universal, standard, or row crop in LPG or gas. This one is a standard LPG model with a narrow front end.

wheels off an old M Farmall toy tractor, the plastic one. The front wheels are two rubber wheels, but they're not the same. There's a little screen on front of the radiator, and whoever built it put a fan blade behind there. It has lights on it, tin can lids for the fenders, and the seat looks like the left or right half of a metal wheel from a metal toy."

The history of that toy intrigues him: Perhaps a child asked for a toy, and a father or grandfather said they would make him one and rooted through the junk drawer, the toy box, or the shop, and sat down and just started crafting it. "The amazing thing is how realistic it is; it looks just like a Moline," Gross says.

One of longtime collector Richard Birklid's favorite farm toys is a scratchbuilt model of an old Buffalo-Pitts tractor built by Albert Steidl of Fingal, North Dakota. "None of those real tractors exist any longer. Albert built one of about 1/16 scale out of pictures

and specs from an original catalog. If you've got eight-foot-high [240-cm] wheels you can scale it down. I kept bugging him, saying I would take it around to shows, that he could sell me half interest in it, but he said he didn't want to sell it. Then one day he came with this tractor—a second one, which I didn't know he was making—and I bought it from him."

Gilbert Berg has been monkeying around with farm toys ever since he was a little kid. In the late 1970s, Berg built a 1/16 Big Bud 747 tractor that ran, and had it auctioned off at the National Farm Toy Show. He had another Big Bud at a friend's table, and the interest in it was so strong from people who wanted to buy it that Berg, a toolmaker, started building them.

His first toys, made of sheet metal, were made after scaling the models off implement dealer booklets or from actual measurements. He decided to fabricate Minneapolis-Moline and Oliver tractors because other

How to Build Farm Toys From Scratch

There are, of course, many methods to building toys from scratch. But if you want a method that's used by someone who regularly scratch-builds toys, here's how:

- Get the real machine's literature and measurements. Implement booklets have lots of details the scratchbuilder needs.
- Take pictures of the real tractor or implement.
- Scale it down by making a blueprint or drawing.
- Make a form of it from aluminum, or cut out brass and form it, which involves bending it with benders and pliers.
- Solder parts together. Don't use glue, which dries quickly and allows parts to come apart easily in just weeks.
- Grind down rough parts until you have achieved the smoothness you want.
- Dip the parts in solvent to clean off the solder flux, fingerprints, and grease.
- Hang it up to dry. A paint booth with heat speeds the process.
- Heat the toy, and then prime it and paint it. "The paint bonds better and dries faster with heat," Gary Van Hove says.
- Hang it up to dry.
- Add tires, decals, and detail parts.

Pete Freiheit John Deere G
Pete Freiheit of Pepin, Wisconsin, scratchbuilt this 1/16 John Deere Hi-Crop G from sand-cast aluminum in 1983. Collection: Eldon Trumm.

tractors with decals present problems to the scratch-builder.

People began to tell him he should make one of these tractors, or one of those, and Berg obliged them. "When people complain about the cost of a tractor, they seldom realize the time you've put into making the molds. One of the tractors I made, well, it took me a year to find the right tractor, and get the statistics and information, before building it. It's not easy."

Berg has scratchbuilt numerous models since 1979. These include 1/64 models of the Minneapolis-Moline G1000, G1000-LP, G900, and G900-LP four-wheel-drive tractors painted in either yellow or red and green. He has also crafted 1/64 Oliver 1850 tractors with narrow-front or wide-front ends, LP gas, and with four-wheel drive with or without cab. In 1/16, he's made the Big Bud—weighing a massive 36 pounds (16.2 kg)—early Steiger four-wheel-drives; Allis-Chalmers 440; International 4156, 4166 with crab steering, 4566, 4 wheel, and A4T; and an Oliver 2655. In addition, he's built a 1/12 and 1/64 Big Bud, and others.

John Janzen of rural Winkler, Manitoba, Canada, says when he was a kid he always had an interest in the farm stuff that was never built. "Ertl made tractors, but not the equipment that went with the tractors," Janzen says. "That was my impetus: To make the equipment to complement the tractors."

Janzen can pinpoint when he got involved in scratchbuilding. "When I was twelve years old, I built a little swather out of wood. It had little wooden wheels and a reel that turned with a small rope. It took me a couple of days to build it and get all the details right so it would run." Following that, Janzen says, whenever he wanted a toy, he made one. "But I didn't make the metal ones until 1982."

Janzen spends 200 to 300 hours a winter on any particular piece that he's building. After scratchbuilding a grain drill, he made a John Deere 2360 swather by welding 18-gauge flat steel, key stock, and 1/8-inch (3-mm) rods together—"Now that's a tough job with those small pieces of steel," he says—and included handmade pulleys. The result is a reel and black silk cloth canvas that turns.

"With a grain drill and swather, then I needed the combine." Thus, he spent another winter planning, cutting, welding, and building a 7721 John Deere pull-type combine. "All the exterior components turn: the pickup header, straw cutter, and the auger, which swings in and out of the hopper."

He uses 9-volt batteries to automate his toys. "The batteries raise and lower the header, move the unloading auger in or out, and just plain turn the whole combine."

Janzen has also made a GMC grain truck with a working hoist, a twelve-row sugar beet planter; a 4440 John Deere with a three-point hitch with Quick-Tatch and an adjustable front axle; a 4620 John Deere out of a 5020; a four-wheel-drive 4386 International tractor he built from scratch; an air seeder; and rock pickers.

Despite his successes, Janzen sometimes has setbacks. "Sometimes I get frustrated. I can't figure out how to do something, or how to make something." Then he puts the work aside for a day or two. "I'll be doing something else, and suddenly the answer will pop into my mind."

He doesn't work on his creations every winter day. "About two or three hours a day when I do, or sometimes eight or ten hours if I'm getting excited."

"The hardest thing in scratchbuilding is welding the little pieces of steel together. The thin pieces have a tendency to warp. I clamp them together in larger pieces of steel to try to prevent that," Janzen says.

"When I've finished one, I have this great sense of accomplishment. It's the greatest feeling in the world; and to have others see them, and make nice comments."

Bob Gray of Eldora, Iowa scratchbuilt his toys with korloy, an aluminum-lead alloy that felt like cast iron, had a similar strength, but had a lower melting point. "They had to make sand-cast molds for that," Gray says. "The kind of metal they make the other kinds of toys out of now was so much quicker and simpler, and they can make so many more toys in a short length of time than they could with this sand-cast deal."

The late Lyle Dingman of Spencer, Iowa, said that quitting his full-time job to go into scratchbuilding farm toys was chancy at first. "You have to build your reputation as a toy maker. Nobody, at the beginning, knows you or your product."

"I want the tractor to be very precise," he said. "You can't just farm a tractor out to someone. We could produce more volume, but they wouldn't be as good. We're not going to sacrifice quality for volume." On the average, Lyle and his wife, Joyce, spent twelve hours making one tractor. "There are some days I'm all thumbs," he said. "I just have to walk away from it." Lyle's methods for scratchbuilding a tractor were

Eldon Trumm John Deere R and 830

Above: *Eldon Trumm produced these 1/16 John Deere tractors in 1983 from sand-cast aluminum. The green tractor is a Model R, the yellow is an 830.*

Terry Rouch John Deere hay loader

Left: *Terry Rouch of Indiana custombuilt this 1/16 John Deere hay loader from die-cast. Collection: Eldon Trumm.*

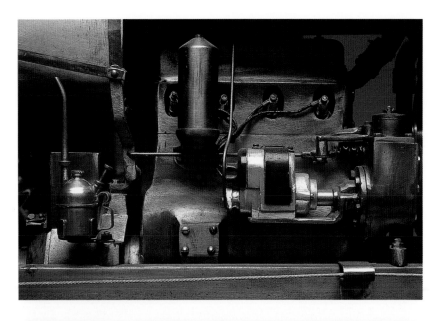

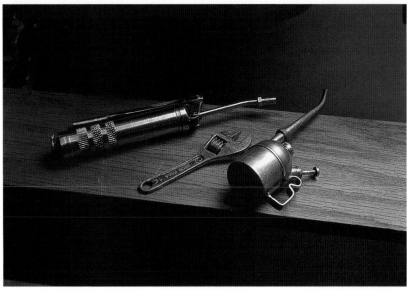

Kermit Ehrenberg Farmall F-20

Above, top: *Notice how realistic the engine, spark plugs, and other side details look on this scratchbuilt steel 1937 Farmall F-20 built by Kermit Ehrenberg of Appleton, Minnesota. Ehrenberg has also built two other 1/4 tractors, a 1938 John Deere C and an 1934 Allis-Chalmers.*

Kermit Ehrenberg Farmall F-20

Above, bottom: *Kermit Ehrenberg scratchbuilt these tools to go along with his 1937 Farmall F-20. The grease gun, wrench, and oil can are all made of steel and are 1/4 size.*

Kermit Ehrenberg Farmall F-20

Right: *Kermit Ehrenberg of Appleton, Minnesota, spent three years and 1,500 hours scratchbuilding this superb 1/4 1937 Farmall F-20 tractor. The only parts that are not handmade are the wheels, which are well-casings, and the differential, which came from a cap cut off of an oxygen tank. The tractor weighs 105 pounds (47 kg).*

Reality and accuracy are what drive the art of customizing farm toys. "Customizing," says Rick Campbell of Apple River, Illinois, "means taking any mass-produced replica but altering it in any way different from the intention of the manufacturer."

There are two types of customizing: "custombuilding," where a builder makes an entirely new tractor out of another tractor by building one's own parts; and "customizing," where one tractor is made into another by changing wheels or adding other stock parts that the builder doesn't make himself.

Custom-building and customizing of farm toys took off in the early days of farm toy collecting, because not enough farm toys of certain types were available; or the toys didn't reflect the actual variations found on real tractors.

A custom-built tractor might involve taking the body of an Ertl tractor, cutting all the details off, and building a new tractor around the Ertl form. "There's a lot more time put into custom-building than straight customizing," Ken Updike says. "In custombuilding, you're actually building it and not just altering it. You're building a lot of the pieces that go onto the tractor body."

Among the best custom-builders is Roger Mohr of Vail, Iowa, who concentrates on just Minneapolis-Molines. Other good custom-builders include Gilson Rieke of Ruthven, Iowa; the late Lyle Dingman of Spencer, Iowa; Gilbert Berg; David Sharp; Vern Eyeman; Rick Campbell of Apple River, Illinois; Wallace Taylor of Burleson, Texas; and Bernie Scott of Cocoa, Florida.

Ron Jenkins of rural Warren, Minnesota, says one of his pet peeves is the name "custom-building," and he prefers to call it "special-building." He says to call it "custom" or "customized" brings up pictures of hot rods with dual exhausts and fancy chrome and the like. "What I want to do is to make a toy tractor look exactly like it did when it was out in the field." To that end, he makes some of his own parts. "We make our own fenders, exhaust stacks, and air cleaners. We buy most of the rest of the parts."

Marvin Fredrick of Oconomowoc, Wisconsin, says his favorites of all the custom-built are the Rieke and Dingman toys. "I've got the Rieke F20 and the plow. When I was on the farm, I had an F20 and that plow, and if it got down to my having to get rid of everything in all my collections some day—which would take about three days, I think—these custom pieces are the ones I'd get rid of last."

Like other custom-builders, Pete Freheit of Red Wing, Minnesota, was thinking about costs of farm tractors when he started customizing. "I started to buy a few tractors to add to the few from my childhood." Then he ran into a typical collector's dilemma: He couldn't find all the tractors he wanted—they were too expensive, or the toys didn't have all the options and details of the actual tractors—so he made his own.

"I had always been good with my hands. I worked in a foundry for ten years. I was always customizing something for my son. I made him a seven-bottom steel plow. A little later I made that Super MTA out of three tractors and finished it off, using Burkholder decals." He showed the finished product to a few guys. "They liked it."

Straight customizing means altering parts that are already on the tractor or adding bought parts, like front-end weights and the like, but not building one's own parts.

Most customizing is probably of farm toy tractors. Al Van Kley of Ankeny, Iowa, says one of his big sellers in customized toys has been a 1/64 toy tractor with saddle tanks. "We take a standard couple-of-dollar tractor, put saddle tanks on, spacer duals, and front assist with fenders. We upgrade the Ertl tractors and try to make them nicer."

Like most facets of farm toys, the attraction is fueled by the real farm vehicles or toys a person grew up with. Lyle Hovland of Rothsay, Minnesota, says he customized a cab for a John Deere 6030 that he had as a kid, using the cab from a 7520, and added a three-point hitch, front weights, "and details that would make it more like real." He's also redone a Caterpillar, adding a V-plow, wing, and cab, "typical of winter road equipment around here. For thirty years, I've watched them go by our farm." Rick Campbell has also customized some toys himself, such as the older 56-66-86 International Harvester series tractors. "I've customized numerous of those over the years."

Gerald Geris of Nelson, Minnesota, says one of the favorite tractors he's customized is a John Deere Model A with a single front wheel. He used an Ertl model, stripped it, and added steel wheels and other items.

"I really got interested in customizing when I saw how the tractor exhausts were made. I didn't like them, so I decided to make my own. And you know how it goes. One thing leads to another." Pretty soon he was making clutches, brakes, air breathers, all the stuff he needed. "I wanted the tractors to look decent."

Not all customizing work is done on tractors. Some of the farm toys Ron Eliason has customized include combines, like a John Deere 6601 prototype he built out of 6600 headers, and an IH 914 prototype combine. He has also worked on tractors, like the Oliver row-crop 77 on which he customized the front end. He also customized an IH 766 into a narrow front from a 966 and an IH 1568 with a cab out of a 1466.

Once Ken Updike and his brothers of Evansville, Wisconsin, figured out how farm toys were constructed, they began altering them. "We had toys that had single rear wheels that we made duals. We took combines and made the heads removable, and took the grain heads and switched them to corn heads.

"One of my earlier customized toys was an Ertl IH 7488. I actually took two tractors to build it. The front half is from a 7488, and the back is a 5288, both Ertls. The reason I built it was that the stock Ertl rear half was incorrect anatomically and appearance-wise, and I just wanted to have one that looked right. I wish they would still make that tractor in real life."

Jerrold Sundstrom of Oriska, North Dakota, says customizers and custom-builders keep outdoing themselves. "When you see some of these custom-built pieces, with all the detail on them, you can't understand how they can sell them so cheaply. You almost can't argue the price people ask. You know how much work has gone into them. There seems to be no end to what they can do."

slightly different than a lot of people's. "First I pick a tractor I have a fond memory of," he said. "When we were kids, everyone worked out on everybody else's farms, so we all got to try out the different tractors." He remembered the time the first new Farmall H came out. "I hung around at the farmer's place until he let me drive it." Lyle Dingman said he also wanted to make a tractor in scale of one that someone else hasn't done.

For Lyle Dingman, the fun was in making the first few of each new model. "After building twenty-five or thirty, it's work," he said. "You couldn't raise a family on it."

Scratchbuilt toys are more desirable than most farm toys because few of each type are usually built—sometimes they are built to a collector's single custom order. Scratchbuilt toys also often have incredible detail. Some of the most prized scratchbuilt toys are those built by Bob Gray of Eldora, Iowa; Terry Rouch; Pete Freiheit of Pepin, Wisconsin; Gilson Rieke of Ruthven, Iowa; Ev Weber; Gilbert Berg of Brooklyn Park, Minnesota; David Sharp; Dan Gubbels; Wally Hooker; Coleman Wheatley of Shelbyville, Indiana; Paul Stephan's Stephan Manufacturing of Beloit, Wisconsin; Vern Eyeman; Roger Mohr of Vail, Iowa; and others. Wayne Eisele of Waterloo, Iowa, has made several farm toys, including a 1/16 loader to fit a Slik Massey-Harris 44 tractor, in 1950.

Weldon Yoder John Deere 730

Above: *Rarity and price are not always determined by scarcity. This 1/16 John Deere 730 diesel was built by Weldon Yoder and family of New Paris, Indiana, in plastic in 1995. Only 500 were made, yet the tractor is worth less than a hundred dollars in the late 1990s. The decal on the side reads "State of Nebraska, Department of Roads." (Photograph by Bill Vossler)*

Barry Hall with John Deere planter

Right: *Barry Hall of Mulberry, Florida, shows off his eight-row John Deere corn planter that he made out of two four-row John Deere planters. (Photograph by Bill Vossler)*

Brown's Models
John Deere A
Above: *This John Deere A came from a kit offered by Brown's Models of England. Collection: Eldon Trumm.*

Ron Eliason Oliver
combine
Left: *This Oliver 542 combine was scratchbuilt by Ron Eliason of Buxton, North Dakota. (Photograph by Bill Vossler)*

Dale Woodliff Exciter
Dale Woodliff of Kendall, Wisconsin, made this custom-built 1/16 Exciter tractor model. It was modeled after a real Exciter tractor that he built and used in tractor pulls.

Appendix

Dollars and Sense: Farm Toy Prices

People collect for many reasons, and whether the collector thinks it is important to make money collecting farm toys or not, it is important to know what farm toys are worth.

Dick Sonnek of Mapleton, Minnesota, compiles *Dick's Farm Toy Price Guide & Check List*, which is *the* guide to farm toy prices. Sonnek says the largest contributors to the price of a farm toy is scarcity and condition, and "to lesser degrees, desirability and popularity." But condition is the biggest factor. He says a rare toy that is missing parts or one that has been repainted hardly ever keeps its value.

Not all rare toys are desirable, however. Not many Kansas Toy Novelty Company Model D John Deere tractors were made, but it is not a very desirable farm toy. "It has no detail, it's very small, something like a 1/50th, and even though it was made in the early 1930s, not a lot of people want it," Sonnek says. "There are very few in existence, but even if there were a lot, not many people would want it, because it's kind of clunky."

Handmade toys often fall into this same category of rare but not valuable, he says. "There has to be some recognition in publications or photos so a collector is aware a toy is out there and seeks them out. How is one collector five states away going to talk about a toy to another collector who has never seen it?"

Rubber toys may not be as easy to find as metal ones; on the other hand, Sonnek says, they also are not as collectible because of lack of detail and durability.

Fred and Marilyn Fintel wrote in *Yesterdays' Toys With Today's Prices* that people interested in farm toys should study research material as much as possible to learn all about the toys they want to collect and where they're being sold. "Once you have started collecting, stay current with trends and prices by reading books and trade journals."

The Fintels also say collectors should strive for quality rather than quantity. "Someday you may want to resell the toys. You may not realize this as a beginning collector, but in time, and as your knowledge grows and your taste becomes more expensive, you may want to resell those original purchases to upgrade your collection. So right from the start, search for quality. Whether you're buying for your own satisfaction or for future resale, you'll never regret buying the best."

Another salient point is to never throw away the box a toy came in, because toys that are "NIB," or "new in box," are worth considerably more than toys without boxes.

Sonnek says pedal tractors are enjoying a boom in prices. "Where that will end, I don't know."

According to him, there are three kinds of collectors: purists, investors, and speculators. To the purist, price isn't as important as finding and enjoying the model. If the value goes up, fine; if not, they still have something they enjoy. For the investors and speculators, Sonnek offers the following recommendation: "My advice is to buy a toy if you like it, rather than as an investment or for speculation. Who knows what the prices are going to do?"

That said, he adds that going by the past is probably the best way to predict the future of farm toy prices. "The most secure would probably be the John Deere brand toys. They always seem to appreciate in value. The others fluctuate a little more widely up and down, and back up again."

For up-to-date information on farm toy prices, check books like *Dick's Farm Toy Price Guide & Check List*; Dave Nolt's *Farm Toy Price Guide*; as well as the magazines in the field, *Toy Farmer*, *Toy Tractor Times*, *Toy Tractor Classics*, and others.

Farm Toy Price Guides

Dick's Farm Toy Price Guide & Check List
Dick Sonnek
24501 470th Avenue
Mapleton, Minnesota 56065
Web site: http://www.bioptik.com

Farm Toy Price Guide
Dave Nolt
PO Box 553-G
Gap, Pennsylvania 17527

Value Guide and Inventory
Raymond E. Crilley Sr.
1881 Eagley Road
East Springfield, Pennsylvania 16411

Fraud and Misrepresentation

Most farm toy people are honest and trusting. They also believe that everybody else is as trustworthy as they.

Collector Joe Male of Millington, Michigan, says he figures going to a farm toy show is probably a good place to go to borrow some money—or lend some. "I wouldn't be surprised if someone came up to me during a farm toy show, the first or second time I met them, and asked for money, and I wouldn't be surprised if I would lend it to them. It's amazing not only how friendly people are at farm toy shows, but how honest."

During one five-year stretch of business, B&S Parts of Hancock, Minnesota, had only one uncollected check, for fifteen dollars. They also have an unusual arrangement with one collector, which illustrates the concept of honesty in the farm toy world. "There's one guy we owe a couple of hundred dollars," Jim Swenson of B&S says. "When I wrote him a check he said 'I don't need the money. When I see you have a toy that I want, I'll just take it, and you subtract it from my bill." His father, Lyle, says he's "served the public all his life, and farm toy people are first-class."

Although the vast majority of farm toy people are honest, the last years of the 1990s have disabused them of the notion that everybody is as honest as they are. As with any group, there are some dishonest people around; some of the sins committed are sins of commission, some are sins of omission.

One collector relates how he had always trusted people to come to his outdoor shed and see his toys, and that sometimes he would leave people in the shed alone with valuable Arcade and Vindex farm toys while he went into the house to answer the telephone. Shortly after one young man's visit, the collector noticed that several of his Arcade and Vindex toys were missing. Subsequently, those same toys turned up on the market. After some research, the collector discovered they had been sold by the same person who had visited the farm toy shed. And though the collector knew those were his toys—he had owned them for several decades and knew them by sight—he had no proof and no way of punishing the criminal.

Dealers at farm toy shows have discovered that they need to be more vigilant than they used to, because the occasional farm toy or two will disappear from their display tables. "Fewer people are true collectors nowadays than ever before," one man says, "and those are the ones you have to watch out for. They're more interested in money than they are in toys, and that way anything can happen. Including theft."

Sins of omission involve situations where sellers allow buyers to believe that toys are something they aren't, that newly made Hubleys and Arcades, for instance, that came out of old Hubley or Arcade molds, are actually the real thing made years ago. The prospective buyer purchases the tractor for the old Hubley or Arcade price, a considerable difference from the price of a reissued toy.

Rick Campbell says the seller of fake cast-iron farm toys is looking for someone who doesn't know cast-iron toys because it's too hard to pass off a fake to someone who knows iron toys. Someone will bury a newer piece in sand and dirt and make it look rusty and old, trying to catch the novice unawares.

He says some of the Product Miniature toys have been reissued during the last fifteen years using the exact same tooling as original PM toys. "The toys have come out slowly, a few popping up at shows, but not a lot of people know that has happened with some of those, like the plastic Farmall M and the WD Allis-Chalmers." He says he doesn't think whoever remade the PM toy had the tire mold, but did have all body castings and wheels and needed to add tires off an old toy that was banged up. Campbell says if you asked the people who bought the tooling, they'll admit they're reproductions. "But I think it gets filtered down. Somebody gets a couple of them and takes them to a show, and they pass through three or four hands until people don't know what they are any more. It can get tricky, especially in the plastic, because people don't know if it is original or not."

There's also over-the-telephone misrepresentation, Jerrold Sundstrom says. "There's just more misrepresentation of toys than there used to be. Don't get me wrong: There are a lot of great people who sell right over the phone, and you get exactly what you want. But there are some who describe a toy on the phone, and when you get it it's not what he was describing. That's no way to run your business. Plus, it makes the collector begin to mistrust everybody who sells over the phone. If there's something wrong with the piece, the seller should let it be known."

In a telephone twist, Lee Blosser of Orrville, Ohio, says he was refused an order for a farm toy over the telephone. "I asked the dealer to send it COD. The dealer said 'I never got a bad check in my life.' But he didn't understand. I was trying to tell him it wasn't the bad check, it was the merchandise. If I don't get the merchandise, I'm out. He's got my money. I even said I'd pay the COD. It's cheaper than losing $135.

"What I'm trying to say is I don't think anybody should be offended, and dealers shouldn't be disappointed if customers ask to have their toys shipped COD. No one should be offended if someone said 'Sorry, I don't know you.' If it doesn't work, then the carrier is in the bind, right? Dealers should, in my opinion, welcome CODs. It would make everybody happy. COD would be nice. It gets everybody off the hook.

"People I've done business with already I won't ask for COD orders. But it's the individual I don't know."

Lyle Swenson of B&S Parts says what alarms him about the future of toy collecting is reproductions of all the old model tractors that sink the price of the originals. "Take the UB Minneapolis Moline tractor. The reproduction really hurt the original. It was worth $300 before the reproduction came out but only about half that afterwards. That's really a kick to the shins of the collector. I worry. Are the International tractors protected? Or the Allis?"

There are the occasional true fraud and fake toys out there, says Ken Updike. "But say you ordered an original Black Knight old style, and it turned out to be a repaint and you were charged for the original, and you found out.

If you yell about it and rat the guy out, nobody else will do business with him." In that way, the farm toy business polices itself.

An instance of self-policing happened in the mid-1990s when a well-known farm toy person crashed and burned, so to speak, when he was allegedly caught misrepresenting prices of toys he had sold for other people. He was a man who'd had a good reputation until evidence of his misdeeds surfaced. Since then he has effectively been shunned by the farm toy world.

A well-known scratchbuilder had his business essentially yanked from under him because a partner stole money and fled.

Maynard Jensen of Chamberlain, South Dakota, says the practice of toy repairing is less trustworthy than it used to be. "Repainted tractors aren't as valuable, because people are skeptical of what might have been covered up. Maybe it doesn't happen often, but it does happen, and that's made people kind of gun shy."

Sundstrom says, "When toys become big money, as they have, that's when fraud starts to show up. Having toys that are worth money is nice, but it's not nice too if you know what I mean. You start getting into too many more problems."

Farm Toy Shows

Farm toy shows are a way of life around the United States and Canada. Any given monthly issue of *Toy Farmer* magazine lists some one hundred different farm toy shows where interested people can go to find the toys they're looking for, as well as meet with friends from all over and discuss important things like toys, weather, farming, or anything else.

Don Gross of Albert Lea, Minnesota, says, "It's a quality bunch of people that frequent the toy shows and even the antique shows. The dealers and people who congregate in those areas are really honest, common people and always have stories to share. One thing I've really noticed is how many families are involved in farm toys and how well-behaved the kids are."

Joe Large of Owaneco, Illinois, says that in late 1981, they went to their first toy show at Ipava, Illinois, and he and his wife, Nita, were hooked. "I could go to a show every weekend, because I just like meeting new people from all over. I like visiting and finding out how their crops are compared to ours and seeing different things. We used to take a vacation, but we don't any more. The toy shows are kind of our vacation now."

Nita, who works for a law firm, says she likes going to shows because it's something they can do together on weekends. "I don't know as much as Joe does about toys, but I know quite a bit about it. I look forward to going to shows. I like to see the craft stuff too once in a while. Sometimes on an afternoon when not much is going on, and we're in a big city, I might do some shopping. I just enjoy being there at the toy shows.

"We meet the same group of people at different toy shows," she says. "This group goes here, and this one goes there, and we'll all go out maybe on a Saturday evening. Do some room trading [swapping toys in motel rooms, usually the evening before the toy show starts] or eat together coming home from a show."

Auctioneer Maynard Jensen of Chamberlain, South Dakota, wonders how many toy collectors were made because of a snowstorm. "One year I auctioneered a toy show at Howard Johnson's in Sioux Falls. We went there on a Friday, and it started storming. It stormed all Friday and Saturday. There was no traffic in or out of Sioux Falls on Saturday. All we had for toy collectors were the few people who had stayed at the Howard Johnson's.

"I thought the toy auction would be a total disaster, but to my surprise, it wasn't. We had people in suits coming into the toy show, and to the auction, because we were the only entertainment in town. We sold toys to some of them. This was sheer entertainment. It was a party mood, a real fun time. I wonder how many toy collecting careers were started that weekend."

Some collectors think there are too many farm toy shows. Rick Campbell of Apple River, Illinois, is one, figuring when he lived in Madison, Wisconsin, the area seemed flooded with toy shows, which created a hardship for dealers at shows, because the audience is split up in different towns.

Things have changed greatly from the early days when farm shows were rare to today when not a single weekend goes by without a farm toy show somewhere in the United States.

The grandfather of farm toy shows is the annual National Farm Toy Show held in early November in Dyersville, Iowa. It is a spectacle not to be missed. Motel rooms must be booked at least a year in advance because 20,000 people show up for the three-day weekend.

Display tables are set up in several places in Dyersville: in the gymnasium, lunch room, halls, and classrooms of Beckman High School; in the main hall of the National Farm Toy Museum a hundred yards south; in the Commercial Club Park building a half-mile away to the north; and in the Scale Models factory, where they empty out the warehouse and set up vendor tables. "Right next door is the assembly line," Ken Updike says, "and they leave toys in different stages of construction out there like they just went for lunch. It's neat to see how the little stuff gets added at each stage."

During "The National," as it is called, all kinds of farm toys, implements, books, and sideline items—like saw blades with scenes of farm toys painted on them—and much more can be found. Jim Buske from Oakes, North Dakota, makes miniature pitchforks, shovels, gas cans, barrels, and other items that people can add to their miniature farm scenes. The National also has a wide variety of farm scenes and displays, and an auction of toys is held in at each year's show.

A few years ago, eleven-year-old Clayton Hendrix of Liberty, Indiana, who was dying of cancer, was sitting through his first auction, when suddenly he heard his name called by auctioneer Wally Hooker. Clayton, who had trouble with his balance, walked gingerly onto the stage and was presented with a silver-plated John Deere 4960 tractor given to him by Don Slama of Wisconsin. Clayton was speechless and had a grin from ear to ear as he showed off the tractor. His great love was John Deere tractors. "I never expected anything like this," he said.

One of the things that Curt Teigen has always enjoyed about the National is "that you'll see someone go by clutching a really expensive toy and really enjoying themselves. Then somebody will come by with a ten-dollar toy and be enjoying it just as much."

Teigen says he sees a lot of fathers and sons involved in the toy hobby together. "I wish it had been going big when my sons were small. It would have been fun to collect with them," he says wistfully.

Clayton Hendrix said, "I never imagined a big tractor show like this. I've really enjoyed the National and feel really good about being here, looking at all the toys, and thinking if I'm going to buy one or not, and seeing how good of shape they are in, and what kind of quality they have."

President of the First State Bank of LaMoure, North Dakota, Les Nesvig attended the National for the first time several years ago. "Claire and Cathy [Scheibe] have been talking about this show for years," Nesvig says, "And when you get here, the people and the displays and the dollars, well, it's unbelievable. It was hard for me to imagine that people could be so interested in toy collecting and would take this much time off and drive this distance. I started getting the impression at the LaMoure Toy Show of how big this whole thing is. This is for real."

Nesvig says he flew into Dubuque and drove out to Dyersville, arriving before the exhibits had been set up. "The parking lot at Beckman School was empty," he says. "Later I went back to Dubuque to change clothes, came right back, and the parking lot was full."

Farm Toy Shows

National Farm Toy Show
Beckman High School
Dyersville, Iowa
800-533-8293
    Typically held in early November

North Dakota Farm Toy Show
LaMoure School Gymnasium
LaMoure, North Dakota
701-883-5206
    Typically held in June

Summer Farm Toy Show, Inc.
3414 Cherry Lynn Drive
Grand Forks, North Dakota 58201
    Held in Dyersville, Iowa, in June

National Toy Truck'n Construction Show
Dome Center at the Monroe County Fairgrounds
East Henrietta Road & Calkins (Route 15A)
Rochester, New York
800-533-8293
    Typically held in mid-August

Wisconsin Farm Progress Show
Ken Updike
306 East Main Street
Evansville, Wisconsin 53536
608-882-6523

Mankato Farm & Antique Show
Mankato Civic Center
Mankato, Minnesota
Contact Persons: Dick and Marion Sonnek
24501 470th Avenue
Mapleton, Minnesota 56065
507-524-3275
    Typically held in January

Farm Toy Show and Sale
Sarasota National Guard Armory
2890 Ringling Boulevard
Sarasota, Florida
Contact Person: Ephraim Horst
941-955-3928

Lafayette Farm Toy Show
Holiday Inn
Junction I-65 and SR 43
Lafayette, Indiana
317-567-2131
    Typically held in March

Mark Twain Great River Annual Toy Show
Ramada Inn
Hannibal, Missouri
Contact Person: Danny W. Gottman
573-769-3255
Contact Person: Fred C. Layman
816-434-5588
    Typically held in February

Northland Antique Toy Show
Northland Toy Shows, Inc.
2298 Commonwealth Avenue
St. Paul, MN 55108
612-429-9401
    Typically held in May

Gateway Mid-America Toy Show
Airport North Holiday Inn
I-70 and Lindbergh
St. Louis, Missouri
Contact Person: Roy Lee Baker
RR1 Box 88
Shipman, Illinois 62685
618-836-7787
    Typically held in February

Decatur Prise of the Prairie Farm Toy Show
Decatur Holiday Inn
U.S. 36 West and Wykles Road
Decatur, Illinois 62522
Contact Persons: Dary and Diana Burnett
RR 3, Box 188
Decatur, Illinois 62526
217-963-2988
Contact Persons: Calvin and Sandee Elder
1875 East 2975 North Road
Mt. Auburn, Illinois 62547
217-668-2436
    Typically held in January

Ontario Toy Show
Woodstock, Ontario, Canada
    Typically held in August

Toy Show
St.-Damase, Quebec, Canada
    Typically held in August

CTM Jamboree
Tractor Classics (CTM)
Box 489
Rocanville, Saskatchewan S0A 3L0
Canada
    Typically held in mid-summer

Canadian Toy Collectors' Society Show
416-633-7878
    Typically held in October

Show and Tell: Farm Toy Museums

Farm toy people have many more resources available in the 1990s than ever before. There are more companies making farm toys than ever before, as well as more scratchbuilders, customizers, and restorers. In addition, there are more sizes and varieties of toys for the modern farm toy aficionado. There are also more museums of farm toys today than ever before, where people can view and learn about all the farm toys ever made.

The best is the National Farm Toy Museum at 1110 16th Avenue SE in Dyersville, Iowa. The NFTM covers every aspect of farm toys through displays of hundreds of tractors and implements, from Arcade and Vindex, the first Ertl toys to the latest, along with those from Reuhl, Bob Gray, Spec-Cast, Scale Models—the entire gamut of the farm toy field.

The museum also exhibits displays of customized, scratchbuilt, 1/64 scale, and 1/8 scale models, plus shelf models, pedal tractors, tractors, combines, manure spreaders—just about everything.

Private collectors also have museums. Three of the best include the Loren Stier Museum in Belle Plaine, Minnesota, Carlyle Greibrok's Mini-History Farm and County Fair Museum in Austin, Minnesota, and Elmer Duellman's museum in Fountain City, Wisconsin.

Loren Stier has many hard-to-find tractors in his collection at the Loren Stier Museum in Belle Plaine, Minnesota, such as a Waterloo Boy replica made by Charley Cox, of which only nineteen were built, as well as farm scenes decade by decade, and much more.

Carlyle Greibrok of Austin, Minnesota, has added thirteen rooms onto his rural home to contain his thousands of farm toys. He has many other toys too like cars, trucks, as well as a series of dioramas and farm and construction scenes. You have to see Greibrok's Mini-History Farm and County Fair Museum, and especially the farm toy layouts and farm toys, to believe it. He says, "One time, I was late getting back here for a woman who was going through the rooms. My wife took her around, and when I came back, the woman said, 'I want to touch the hand of the genius who did this.'"

Comments like that embarrass him, Greibrok says, but they also give a sense of the scope of what he has done. He has hundreds of farm tractors, implements, and trucks in his collection, as well as thousands of other toys, dioramas, and specially dedicated rooms.

Elmer Duellman of Fountain City, Wisconsin, also has a huge collection of toys. He has only a few 1/16 tractors but has hundreds of pedal tractors. His toy collection is massive and includes just about every toy imaginable in a series of quonsets.

But his joy is his museum. He's so well known in the toy fields that every time he goes somewhere and comes back home, it seems like there's a new package in the mail with a different toy for his museum. "As far as the toys go, I went to auctions and started picking them up cheap, and kept on stacking them up. Sometimes I think I should quit buying them," Duellman says. "But then I don't. It's all just too much fun."

Farm Toy Museums

National Farm Toy Museum
1110 16th Avenue SE
Dyersville, Iowa 52040
319-875-2727

Boone Vindex Museum
Boone County Historical Society Museum
311 Whitney Boulevard
Belvidere, Illinois 61008
815-544-8391

The Boone Vindex Museum contains every Vindex toy officially made and is located within the Boone County Historical Society Museum in Belvidere.

Toy Farmer Museum
7496 106th Avenue SE
LaMoure, North Dakota 58458-9404
701-883-5206

The *Toy Farmer* Museum is located on the farm property belonging to Claire and Cathy Scheibe. It contains a wide variety of farm toys, including all the toys sponsored by *Toy Farmer*.

Greibrok's Mini-History Farm and County Fair Museum
Route 3
Austin, Minnesota 55912
507-433-4880

Elmer's Auto and Toy Museum
W903 Elmer's Road
Fountain City, Wisconsin 54629
608-687-7221

The Farm Museum
PO Box 38
Milton, Ontario, Canada L9T 2YR
905-878-8151

Loren Stier Museum
125 West Park Street
Belle Plaine, Minnesota 56011
612-873-6652

Sources

Besides essential resources like *Toy Farmer*, farm toys are also featured in magazines like *Toy Box, Collecting Toys, Mobilia, Toy Trucker & Contractor*, and others.

Magazines

Toy Farmer
7496 106th Avenue SE
LaMoure, North Dakota 58458-9404
701-883-5206 or 800-533-8293
Fax: 701-883-5209
Web site: http://www.toyfarmer.com

Collecting Toys
Kalmbach Publishing Co.
21027 Crossroads Circle
Waukesha, Wisconsin 53187-1612
414-796-8776
Web site: http://www.toymag.com

Toy Trucker & Contractor
7496 106th Avenue SE
LaMoure, North Dakota 58458-9404
701-883-5206 or 800-533-8293
Fax: 701-883-5209
Web site: http://www.toyfarmer.com

Mobilia
PO Box 515
Middlebury, Vermont 05753
802-388-3071
Fax: 802-388-2215
Web site: http://www.mobilia.com

Toy Shop
Krause Publications
700 East State Street
Iola, Wisconsin 54990-0001
715-445-2214
Fax: 715-445-4087
Web site: http://www.krause.com

Warman's Today's Collector
Krause Publications
700 East State Street
Iola, Wisconsin 54990-0001
715-445-2214
Fax: 715-445-4087
Web site: http://www.krause.com

Toy Tractor Times
Box 156
Osage, Iowa 50461
515-732-3530

Tractor Classics (CTM)
Box 489
Rocanville, Saskatchewan
Canada S0A 3L0
306-645-4566
Fax: 306-645-4566

Recommended Reading

Caney, Steven. *Toy Book*. New York: Workman Publishing Co., 1972.

Crilley, Raymond E., Sr., and Charles E. Burkholder. *Collecting Model Farm Toys of the World*. Tucson, Arizona: Aztex, 1979.

Crilley, Raymond E., Sr., and Charles E. Burkholder. *International Director of Model Farm Tractors & Implements*. Atglen, Pennsylvania: Schiffer, 1985.

Doucette, Joseph, and C. L. Collins. *Collecting Antique Toys*. New York: Macmillan Publishing Co., Inc., 1981.

Gottschalk, Lillian. *American Toy Cars & Trucks*. New York: Abbeville Press, 1985.

Hertz, Louis. *The Toy Collector*. New York: Funk & Wagnalls, 1969.

Hughes, Ralph C. *The Toy and the Real McCoy*. Moline, Illinois: Deere & Company Service Publications, 1990.

Huxford, Sharon, and Bob Huxford, eds. *Shroeder's Collectible Toys Antique to Modern Price Guide*. Collector Books, Schroeder Publishing Co., Inc., 1995.

Ketchum, William C., Jr. *Toys and Games*. Washington, D. C.: The Smithsonian Institution, 1981.

Korbeck, Sharon, ed. *Toys & Prices*. 5th edition. Iola, Wisconsin: Krause Publications, 1997.

Longest, David. *Toys, Antique & Collectible*. Paducah, Kentucky: Collector Books, 1995.

O'Brien, Richard. *The Story of American Toys*. New York: Artabras (Abbeville Press), 1990.

Pinsky, Maxine A. *Marx Toys: Robots, Space, Comic, Disney & TV Characters*. Atglen, Pennsylvania: Schiffer, 1996.

Schroeder, Joseph J., Jr., ed. *Toys, Games & Dolls 1860–1930*. Northfield, Illinois: Digest Books, Inc.

Sonnek, Dick. *Dick's Farm Toy Price Guide & Check List*. Mapleton, Minnesota, n.p., n.d.

Spero, James, ed. *Collectible Toys and Games of the Twenties and Thirties from Sears, Roebuck and Co. Catalogs*. New York: Dover Publications, 1988.

Trumm, Eldon, and Robert Zarse. *A Guide to Collecting John Deere Farm & Construction Toys*. Worthington, Iowa, n.p., n.d.

Trumm, Eldon, and Robert Zarse. *Encyclopedia of Farm and Construction Toys*. N.p., n.d.

Trumm, Eldon, and Robert Zarse. *Ertl and Toy Tractors*. Volumes 1 and 2. N.p., n.d. [1986—1987].

Wagner, Robert, and Vincent Manocchi. *Toy Tractors*. Osceola, Wisconsin: Motorbooks International, 1996.

White, Gwen. *Antique Toys and Their Background*. New York: Arco Publishing Co., 1971.

Whitton, Blair. *Toys: The Knopf Collectors' Guides to American Antiques*. New York: Chanticleer Press, Alfred A. Knopf, 1984.

Zarse, Robert. *A Guide to Collecting McCormick and International Toys*. N.p., n.d. [1984].

Zarse, Robert. *On the International Scene*. N.p., n.d. [1982].

Index

About the Author and Photographer

Bill Vossler has written about farm toys, collectors, and toy makers since 1985, and is a regular contributor to *Toy Farmer* magazine.

His book *Burma-Shave: The Rhymes, The Signs, The Times* was nominated for a Minnesota Book Award. He also contributed to *This Old Tractor* (Voyageur Press) and is the author of *Orphan Tractors*. In addition to three published books, the author has published 2,200 articles, essays, short stories, poems, and a play in 150 different magazines, including *Reader's Digest, Chicago Times Magazine, Toy Trucker & Contractor, Red Power, Polk's Antique Tractor Magazine*, and many more.

He lives in Rockville, Minnesota, with his wife, Nicolyn Rajala, and their cat, Mittens.